CONSUMER MATH
SOLUTION KEY
CONTENTS

SECTION KEY

SELF TEST KEY

TEST KEY

Alpha Omega Publications®

804 N. 2nd Ave. E., Rock Rapids, IA 51246-1759

SUGGESTIONS FOR SOLUTION KEY USAGE

This Math Solution Key contains the step-by-step procedures necessary to solve each Section activity and Self Test problem. The solutions are patterned after the models in the LIFEPACs. However, alternative solutions are often possible and other methods may be used.

The Solution Key is designed to be used by the teacher and student as a resource when the answer in the Answer Key can not be found or when the solution method is not evident. However, excessive reliance on the Solution Key can diminish the learning of the knowledge and reduce the retention of the principles which are necessary to successfully complete the Self Tests and LIFEPAC Tests.

CONSUMER MATHEMATICS 1
SOLUTION KEY

I. SECTION ONE

1.1

+	5	2	1	7	6	3	4	8	9
7	12	9	8	14	13	10	11	15	16
3	8	5	4	10	9	6	7	11	12
8	13	10	9	15	14	11	12	16	17
2	7	4	3	9	8	5	6	10	11
9	14	11	10	16	15	12	13	17	18
1	6	3	2	8	7	4	5	9	10
4	9	6	5	11	10	7	8	12	13
5	10	7	6	12	11	8	9	13	14
6	11	8	7	13	12	9	10	14	15

1.2 7

1.3 17

1.4 27

1.5 37

1.6 10

1.7 20

1.8 30

1.9 60

1.10 12

1.11 22

1.12 32

1.13 82

1.14 11

1.15 21

1.16 31

1.17 51

1.18 80

1.19 81

1.20 82

1.21 83

1.22 90

1.23 91

1.24 92

1.25 93

1.26 100

1.27 101

1.28 102

1.29 103

1.30 100

1.31 101

1.32 102

1.33 103

1.34 13

1.35 15

1.36 12

1.37 14

1.38 9

1.39 17

1.40 19

1.41 19

1.42 21

1.43 17

1.44 23

1.45 26

1.46	24
1.47	27
1.48	22
1.49	31
1.50	29
1.51	32
1.52	32
1.53	29
1.54	55
1.55	59
1.56	93
1.57	62
1.58	23
1.59	29
1.60	33
1.61	33
1.62	29
1.63	28
1.64	32
1.65	31
1.66	89
1.67	79
1.68	87
1.69	62
1.70	102
1.71	105
1.72	89
1.73	87
1.74	75
1.75	75
1.76	181
1.77	136
1.78	71
1.79	90
1.80	125
1.81	77
1.82	100
1.83	112
1.84	794
1.85	643
1.86	265
1.87	312
1.88	293
1.89	844
1.90	703
1.91	305
1.92	402
1.93	363
1.94	1,444
1.95	1,503
1.96	705
1.97	1,002
1.98	863
1.99	1,444
1.100	1,503
1.101	3

1.102 13

1.103 23

1.104 33

1.105 3

1.106 13

1.107 23

1.108 53

1.109 8

1.110 18

1.111 28

1.112 48

1.113 5

1.114 15

1.115 35

1.116 75

1.117 20

1.118 19

1.119 18

1.120 40

1.121 39

1.122 38

1.123 70

1.124 69

1.125 68

1.126 90

1.127 89

1.128 88

1.129 43

1.130 56

1.131 34

1.132 7

1.133 19

1.134 41

1.135 50

1.136 31

1.137 34

1.138 18

1.139 35

1.140 48

1.141 49

1.142 67

1.143 11

1.144 533

1.145 513

1.146 747

1.147 704

1.148 808

1.149 521

1.150 798

1.151 738

1.152 406

1.153 319

1.154 410

1.155 174

1.156 466

1.157 45

1.158 414

1.159 349

1.160 412

1.161 234

1.162 338

1.163 197

1.164 168

1.165 54

1.166 1,771

1.167 2,782

1.168 1,877

1.169 3,906

1.170 66,037

1.171 2,725

1.172 806

1.173 2,061

1.174 1,766

1.175 18,989

1.176

x	3	0	2	6	4	9	7	1	8	5
1	3	0	2	6	4	9	7	1	8	5
5	15	0	10	30	20	45	35	5	40	25
3	9	0	6	18	12	27	21	3	24	15
9	27	0	18	54	36	81	63	9	72	45
8	24	0	16	48	32	72	56	8	64	40
6	18	0	12	36	24	54	42	6	48	30
2	6	0	4	12	8	18	14	2	16	10
4	12	0	8	24	16	36	28	4	32	20
7	21	0	14	42	28	63	49	7	56	35
0	0	0	0	0	0	0	0	0	0	0

1.177 180

1.178 368

1.179 729

1.180 108

1.181 216

1.182 124

1.183 360

1.184 568

1.185 279

1.186 328

1.187 637

1.188 106

1.189 48

1.190 216

1.191 161

1.192 175

1.193 666

1.194 704

1.195 315

1.196 584

1.197 285

1.198 558

1.199 340

1.200 696

1.201 384

1.202 228

1.203 392

1.204 290

1.205 102

1.206 144

1.207 756

1.208 396

1.209 78

1.210 114

1.211 288

1.212 273

1.213 2,583

1.214 3,132

1.215 37,488

1.216 27,852

1.217 24,836

1.218 5,652

1.219 4,195

2.220 26,033

1.221 66,536

1.222 35,180

1.223 320

1.224 1,080

1.225 920

1.226 2,100

1.227 740

1.228 2,640

1.229
16
23
48
32
368

1.230
54
24
216
108
1296

1.231
23
47
161
92
1081

1.232
35
65
175
210
2275

1.233
74
19
666
74
1406

1.234
88
38
704
264
3344

1.235
74
39
666
222
2886

1.236
58
17
406
58
986

1.237
64
27
448
128
1728

1.238
68
91
68
612
6188

```
1.239      81
           42
          162
         324
         3402
```

```
1.240      75
           23
          225
         150
         1725
```

```
1.241      38
           45
          190
         152
         1710
```

```
1.242     39
          25
         195
         78
         975
```

```
1.243      36
           28
          288
          72
         1008
```

```
1.244      47
           26
          282
          94
         1222
```

```
1.245      76
           63
          228
         456
         4788
```

```
1.246      69
           56
          414
         345
         3864
```

```
1.247      486
            21
           486
          972
         10206
```

```
1.248     213
          165
         1065
        1278
        213
        35145
```

```
1.249      198
           751
           198
          990
        1386
        148698
```

```
1.250      872
           534
          3488
         2616
        4360
        465648
```

```
1.251      7204
            618
          57632
          7204
        43224
        4452072
```

```
1.252     673
           46
         4038
        2692
        30958
```

```
1.253    109
          23
         327
        218
        2507
```

```
1.254     134
          649
         1206
         536
        804
        86966
```

```
1.255     451
          107
         3157
        451
        48257
```

1.256
```
    3,192
      823
     9576
    6384
  25536
2,627,016
```

1.257
```
     4 R2
  6)26
    24
     2
```

1.258
```
     6 R2
  5)32
    30
     2
```

1.259
```
     4 R4
  9)40
    36
     4
```

1.260
```
     6 R5
  6)41
    36
     5
```

1.261
```
     8 R2
  8)66
    64
     2
```

1.262
```
     4 R3
  7)31
    28
     3
```

1.263
```
     9 R1
  3)28
    27
     1
```

1.264
```
     3 R3
  8)27
    24
     3
```

1.265
```
     5 R3
  7)38
    35
     3
```

1.266
```
     8 R8
  9)80
    72
     8
```

1.267
```
    249 R1
  3)748
    6
    14
    12
     28
     27
      1
```

1.268
```
    206 R3
  4)827
    8
    027
     24
      3
```

1.269
```
    120 R4
  5)604
    5
    10
    10
     04
```

1.270
```
    134
  7)938
    7
    23
    21
     28
     28
      0
```

1.271
```
     44 R5
  8)357
    32
     37
     32
      5
```

1.272
```
    128
  6)768
    6
    16
    12
     48
     48
      0
```

```
         117 R4
1.273  8)940
         8
         14
          8
          60
          56
           4
```

```
          58 R1
1.274  2)117
         10
          17
          16
           1
```

```
          98 R1
1.275  5)491
         45
          41
          40
           1
```

```
          93 R2
1.276  9)839
         81
          29
          27
           2
```

```
         157 R1
1.277  3)472
         3
         17
         15
          22
          21
           1
```

```
          79 R5
1.278  6)479
         42
          59
          54
           5
```

```
          98 R5
1.279  8)789
         72
          69
          64
           5
```

```
         208 R2
1.280  4)834
         8
         034
          32
           2
```

```
         121 R1
1.281  6)727
         6
         12
         12
          07
           6
           1
```

```
          95 R2
1.282  3)287
         27
          17
          15
           2
```

```
          66 R3
1.283  4)267
         24
          27
          24
           3
```

```
          97 R1
1.284  7)680
         63
          50
          49
           1
```

```
          96 R8
1.285  9)872
         81
          62
          54
           8
```

```
         233 R2
1.286  4)934
         8
         13
         12
          14
          12
           2
```

```
1.287     124 R4
        5)624
          5
          12
          10
           24
           20
            4
```

```
1.288      65 R1
        9)586
          54
           46
           45
            1
```

```
1.289      79 R1
        3)238
          21
           28
           27
            1
```

```
1.290     263 R2
        3)791
          6
          19
          18
           11
            9
            2
```

```
1.291     142 R4
        7)998
          7
          29
          28
           18
           14
            4
```

```
1.292     164 R1
        4)657
          4
          25
          24
           17
           16
            1
```

```
1.293     118 R3
        8)947
          8
          14
           8
           67
           64
            3
```

```
1.294     235 R1
        3)706
          6
          10
           9
           16
           15
            1
```

```
1.295     135 R2
        7)947
          7
          24
          21
           37
           35
            2
```

```
1.296     137 R5
        6)827
          6
          22
          18
           47
           42
            5
```

```
1.297     101 R2
        7)709
          7
          009
            7
            2
```

```
1.298      94 R3
        5)473
          45
           23
           20
            3
```

```
1.299     106 R1
        4)425
          4
          025
           24
            1
```

1.300
```
  108 R2
9)974
  9
  074
   72
    2
```

1.301
```
   63 R3
9)570
  54
   30
   27
    3
```

1.302
```
  247 R2
3)743
  6
  14
  12
   23
   21
    2
```

1.303
```
   81 R3
4)327
  32
   07
    4
    3
```

1.304
```
  136 R4
5)684
  5
  18
  15
   34
   30
    4
```

1.305
```
  130 R4
7)914
  7
  21
  21
   04
```

1.306
```
   82 R2
8)658
  64
   18
   16
    2
```

1.307
```
  128 R1
6)769
  6
  16
  12
   49
   48
    1
```

1.308
```
  117 R5
8)941
  8
  14
   8
   61
   56
    5
```

1.309
```
  208 R1
2)417
  4
  017
   16
    1
```

1.310
```
  158 R1
5)791
  5
  29
  25
   41
   40
    1
```

1.311
```
   80 R6
9)726
  72
   06
```

II. SECTION TWO

2.1 Since the digits are odd, they must be 1, 3, 5, 7, or 9.

If the last two digits add to make 10, they must be 1 and 9, 3 and 7, or 5 and 5.

If the first and last digits add to make 8, they must be 1 and 7 or 3 and 5.

2.1 cont.

So far the possible combinations are

	~~1~~	~~9~~
7	9	1
1	3	7
5	7	3
3	5	5

Since 9 is larger than 8, the 1 and then 9 can be crossed out.

If the first two digits add to make 12, they must be 3 and 9 or 5 and 7.

The only combination whose first two digits add to make 12 is 573. Therefore, S is 573.

2.2 The numbers that add to make 20 are 1 and 19, 2 and 18, 3 and 17, 4 and 16, 5 and 15, 6 and 14, 7 and 13, 8 and 12, 9 and 11, and 10 and 10. The two numbers that have a difference of 4 are 8 and 12.

2.3 12, 24

2.4 Across
1. 1533
2. 5 x 3239 = 16195

Down
1. 173 + 1533 = 1706
3. 1533 + 1706 = 3239

2.5 through 2.12

Rectangle stamps:
2.8, 2.9, and 2.11 = 24¢

Rectangle stamps with animals:
2.8 and 2.11 = 16¢

2.5 through 2.12 cont.

Triangle stamps:
2.10 and 2.12 = 24¢

Square stamps:
2.5, 2.6, and 2.7 = 11¢

Stamps with animals:
2.6, 2.8, and 2.11 = 20¢

Stamps with two animals:
2.6 and 2.11 = 13¢

Stamps with a person:
2.9 and 2.12 = 22¢

Stamps with mechanical devices:
2.5, 2.9, and 2.10 = 20¢

Stamp 2.9 = 24¢ - 16¢ = 8¢

Stamp 2.12 = 22¢ - Stamp 2.9
= 22¢ - 8¢
= 14¢

Stamp 2.10 = 24¢ - Stamp 2.12
= 24¢ - 14¢
= 10¢

Stamp 2.5 = 20¢ - (Stamp 2.9 + Stamp 2.10)
= 20¢ - (8¢ + 10¢)
= 20¢ - 18¢
= 2¢

Stamp 2.6 = 20¢ - (Stamp 2.8 + Stamp 2.11)
= 20¢ - 16¢
= 4¢

Stamp 2.7 = 11¢ - (Stamp 2.5 + Stamp 2.6)
= 11¢ - (2¢ + 4¢)
= 11¢ - 6¢
= 5¢

Stamp 2.11 = 13¢ - Stamp 2.6
= 13¢ - 4¢
= 9¢

Stamp 2.8 = 16¢ - Stamp 2.11
= 16¢ - 9¢
= 7¢

2.13 true

2.14 false

2.15 true

2.16 true

2.17 false

2.18 false

2.19 true

2.20 true

2.21 through 2.30 Examples:

2.21 1, 2, 3, 4, 6, 8, 12, or 24

2.22 1, 2, 3, 4, 6, 8, 12, or 24

2.23 1, 2, 4, 7, 14, or 28

2.24 1, 3, 11, or 33

2.25 1, 2, 4, 8, 16, 32, or 64

2.26 4, 8, 12, . . .

2.27 15, 30, 45, . . .

2.28 1, 7, 11, or 77

2.29
a. 1, 2, 4, 8, 16, 32, or 64
b. 1, 2, 4, 8, 16, 32, or 64

2.30 63, 126, 189, . . .

2.31 true

2.32 true

2.33 false

2.34 true

2.35 true

2.36 false

2.37 false

2.38 true

2.39 true

2.40 Any order:
a. 1
b. 3
c. 5
d. 15

2.41 Any order:
a. 1
b. 2
c. 4
d. 5
e. 10
f. 20

2.42 31 or 37

2.43 41 or 43

2.44 47

2.45 2, 7

2.46 Any order:
a. 2
b. 5

2.47 Any order:
a. 2
b. 3
c. 5

2.48 5

2.49 The factors of 28 are 1, 2, 4, 7, 14, and 28.
The prime factors are 2 and 7, of which 7 is the largest.

2.50 The factors of 24 are 1, 2, 3, 4, 6, 8, 12, and 24.
The prime factors are 2 and 3, of which 3 is the largest.

2.51 The factors of 7 are 1 and 7. The largest prime factor is 7.

2.52 The factors of 33 are 1, 3, 11, and 33. The prime factors are 3 and 11, of which 11 is the largest.

2.53 The factors of 34 are 1, 2, 17, and 34. The prime factors are 2 and 17, of which 17 is the largest.

2.54 The factors of 32 are 1, 2, 4, 8, 16, and 32. The largest prime factor is 2.

III. SECTION THREE

3.1
$$\begin{array}{r} 796 \\ 3{,}486 \\ +\ 56{,}975 \\ \hline 61{,}257 \end{array}$$

3.2
$$\begin{array}{r} 364 \\ +\ 289 \\ \hline 653 \end{array}$$

3.3
$$\begin{array}{r} 184 \\ +\ 348 \\ \hline 532 \end{array}$$

3.4
$$\begin{array}{r} 312 \\ 431 \\ +\ 551 \\ \hline 1{,}294 \end{array}$$

3.5
$$\begin{array}{r} 167 \\ 208 \\ +\ 221 \\ \hline 596 \end{array}$$

3.6
$$\begin{array}{r} 587 \\ -\ 104 \\ \hline 483 \end{array}$$

3.7
$$\begin{array}{r} 596 \\ -\ 280 \\ \hline 316 \end{array}$$

3.8
$$\begin{array}{r} 764 \\ -\ 443 \\ \hline 321 \end{array}$$

3.9
$$\begin{array}{r} 829 \\ -\ 564 \\ \hline 265 \end{array}$$

3.10
$$\begin{array}{r} 213 \\ 462 \\ 381 \\ +\ 296 \\ \hline 1{,}352 \end{array}$$

3.11
$$\begin{array}{r} 877 \\ -\ 382 \\ \hline 495 \end{array}$$

3.12
$$\begin{array}{r} 6{,}118 \\ -\ 2{,}873 \\ \hline 3{,}245 \end{array}$$

3.13
$$\begin{array}{r} 234 \\ -\ 186 \\ \hline 48 \end{array}$$

3.14
$$\begin{array}{r} 39 \\ +\ 57 \\ \hline 96 \end{array}$$

3.15
$$\begin{array}{r} \$\ 438 \\ +\ 938 \\ \hline \$1{,}376 \end{array} \qquad \begin{array}{r} \$3{,}468 \\ -\ 1{,}376 \\ \hline \$2{,}092 \end{array}$$

3.16
$$\begin{array}{r} 684 \\ +\ 279 \\ \hline 963 \end{array}$$

3.17
$$\begin{array}{r} 2{,}876 \\ +\ 5{,}491 \\ \hline 8{,}367 \end{array}$$

3.18
$$\begin{array}{r} 2{,}139 \\ 8{,}476 \\ +\ 9{,}347 \\ \hline 19{,}962 \end{array}$$

3.19
$$\begin{array}{r} 877 \\ -\ 648 \\ \hline 229 \end{array}$$

3.20
$$\begin{array}{r} 6{,}542 \\ -\ 4{,}658 \\ \hline 1{,}884 \end{array}$$

3.21 $\begin{array}{r} 7,264 \\ -\ 5,837 \\ \hline 1,427 \end{array}$

3.22 $\begin{array}{r} 19 \\ \times\ 46 \\ \hline 114 \\ 76\ \\ \hline 874 \end{array}$

3.23 $\begin{array}{r} 34 \\ \times\ 23 \\ \hline 102 \\ 68\ \\ \hline 782 \end{array}$

3.24 $\begin{array}{r} 24 \\ \times\ 36 \\ \hline 144 \\ 72\ \\ \hline 864 \end{array}$

3.25
a. $\begin{array}{r} 57 \\ \times\ \ 2 \\ \hline 114 \end{array}$

b. $\begin{array}{r} 57 \\ \times\ \ 3 \\ \hline 171 \end{array}$

c. $\begin{array}{r} 57 \\ \times\ \ 7 \\ \hline 399 \end{array}$

3.26
a. 52

b. $\begin{array}{r} 52 \\ \times\ \ 2 \\ \hline 104 \end{array}$

c. $\begin{array}{r} 52 \\ \times\ 12 \\ \hline 104 \\ 52\ \\ \hline 624 \end{array}$

d. $\begin{array}{r} 52 \\ \times\ 27 \\ \hline 364 \\ 104\ \\ \hline 1,404 \end{array}$

e. $\begin{array}{r} 146 \\ \times\ \ 52 \\ \hline 292 \\ 730\ \\ \hline 7,592 \end{array}$

3.27 $\begin{array}{r} 17 \\ \times\ \ 8 \\ \hline 136 \end{array}$

3.28 6 x 9 x 1 = 54

3.29 9 x 13 x 1 = 117

3.30 1 x 20 x 14 = 280

3.31 2 x 20 x 14 = 560

3.32 2 x 17 x 1 = 34

3.33 2 x 17 x 2 = 68

3.34 2 x 17 x 3 = 102

3.35 2 x 17 x 9 = 306

3.36 8 x 7 x 1 = 56

3.37 8 x 7 x 3 = 168

3.38 1 x 14 x 15 = 210

3.39 2 x 14 x 15 = 420

3.40 9 x 14 x 15 = 1,890

3.41 $\begin{array}{r} 37 \\ \times\ 29 \\ \hline 333 \\ 74\ \\ \hline 1,073 \end{array}$

3.42 $\begin{array}{r} 414 \\ \times\ \ 23 \\ \hline 1242 \\ 828\ \\ \hline 9,522 \end{array}$

3.43 $\begin{array}{r} 34 \\ \times\ 28 \\ \hline 272 \\ 68\ \\ \hline 952 \end{array}$

3.44 $\begin{array}{r} 281 \\ \times\ \ 91 \\ \hline 281 \\ 2529\ \\ \hline 25,571 \end{array}$

3.45

```
   834
 x 612
  1668
  834
5004
510,408
```

3.46 Since Q is divisible by 15, the last digit must be 5.

For the first two digits to add to 10, they must be 1 and 9 or 3 and 7.

For the second and third digits to add to 14, since the third digit is 5, the second digit must be 9.

If the second digit is 9 the first digit must be 1.

Therefore, Q = 915.

a. 1
b. 9
c. 5

3.47

```
   35 R4
7)249
  21
   39
   35
    4
```

3.48

```
   74 R8
9)674
  63
   44
   36
    8
```

3.49 896 ÷ 112 = 8

3.50

```
    184 R 26
27)4,994
   27
   229
   216
    134
    108
     26
```

3.51 a.

```
     14 R3
30)423
   30
   123
   120
     3
```

b. 3

3.52 a.

```
   53 R2
5)267
  25
   17
   15
    2
```

b. 2

3.53

```
   42 R1
9)379
  36
   19
   18
    1
```

3.54

```
   48 R3
6)291
  24
   51
   48
    3
```

3.55

```
   82 R1
6)493
  48
   13
   12
    1
```

3.56

```
    173 R15
39)6,762
   39
   286
   273
    132
    117
     15
```

3.57 a. 52
b. 104 ÷ 52 = 2
c. 208 ÷ 52 = 4
d. 364 ÷ 52 = 7
e. 624 ÷ 52 = 12
f. 1,976 ÷ 52 = 38

3.58
6,202
4,563
+ 7,349
18,114

3.59
2,261
4,982
+ 9,474
16,717

3.60
234
17)3,978
34
57
51
68
68
0

3.61
9
137)1,233
1233
0

3.62
28
37)1,036
74
296
296
0

3.63
6 x 1 = 6
54 ÷ 6 = 9

3.64
7 x 1 = 7
154 ÷ 7 = 22

3.65
9 x 14 x 1 = 126

3.66
17 x 1 = 17
102 ÷ 17 = 6

3.67
217
361
298
+ 847
1,723

3.68
66 R6
7)468
42
48
42
6

3.69
647
856
925
+ 789
3,217

3.70
14
87)1,218
87
348
348
0

3.71
13
6)78
6
18
18
0

3.72
19
6)114
6
54
54
0

3.73
112
39)4,368
39
46
39
78
78
0

3.74
a. 4 x 6 = 24
b. 24 x 4 = 96

3.75
a. 6 x 3 = 18
b. 5 x 3 = 15
c. 3 pencils = 3 x 6 =
18 paper clips
18 + 4 = 22 paperclips
22 x 3 = 66 matches
d. 2 pencils = 2 x 6 =
12 paper clips
9 matches = 9 ÷ 3 =
3 paper clips
12 + 3 = 15 paper clips

3.76
less than
12 matches = 12 ÷ 3 =
4 paper clips
2 pencils = 2 x 6 =
12 paper clips
12 + 1 = 13 paper clips

3.77 more than
3 pencils = 3 x 6 =
18 paper clips

3.78 more than
2 pencils = 2 x 6 =
12 paper clips
12 + 2 = 14 paper clips
14 paper clips = 14 x 3 =
42 matches

3.79 less than
22 paper clips = 22 x 3 =
66 matches

3.80 more than
5 pencils = 5 x 6 =
30 paper clips
30 paper clips = 30 x 3 =
90 matches
90 + 2 = 92 matches

3.81 7 + 8 = 15
15 + 4 = 19
19 - 9 = 10

3.82 47 - 9 = 38
38 + 6 = 44
44 - 8 = 36
36 + 3 = 39
39 - 7 = 32

3.83 11 + 7 = 18
18 - 9 = 9
9 + 6 = 15
15 - 4 = 11
11 + 9 = 20

3.84 28 + 31 = 59

3.85 46 + 12 = 58
58 + 8 = 66

3.86 32 - 5 = 27
27 + 7 = 34
34 + 8 = 42
42 - 6 = 36

3.87 53 + 25 = 78
78 - 9 = 69

3.88 320 x 5 = 1,600

3.89 152 x 7 = 1,064 for two motorcycles
1,064 ÷ 2 = 532

3.90
a. 49 x 5 = 245
b. 245 x 7 = 1,715

3.91
a. 2 red chips = 2 x 4 =
8 white chips
1 blue chip = 7 white chips
8 + 7 = 15 white chips
b. 3 red chips = 3 x 4 =
12 white chips
2 blue chips = 2 x 7 =
14 white chips
12 + 14 = 26 white chips

3.92
a. 1 purple chip =
2 x 6 = 12 white chips
b. 3 purple chips =
3 x 2 = 6 orange chips
6 orange chips =
6 x 6 = 36 white chips
c. 24 white chips =
24 ÷ 6 = 4 orange chips
d. 38 orange chips =
38 ÷ 2 = 19 purple chips

3.93 5 x 7 x 3 = 105

CONSUMER MATHEMATICS 2
SOLUTION KEY

I. SECTION ONE

1.1 Example:
a symbol consisting of a bar, a whole number above the bar, and a whole number below the bar

1.2 Example:
the number above the bar in a fraction

1.3 Example:
the number below the bar in a fraction

1.4 through 1.6, Any order:

1.4 a part of a whole

1.5 a division

1.6 a ratio

1.7 proper

1.8 mixed

1.9 improper

1.10 proper

1.11 improper

1.12 1

1.13 Examples:
a. $\frac{1}{3} = \frac{1 \times 2}{3 \times 2} = \frac{2}{6}$
b. $\frac{1}{3} = \frac{1 \times 10}{3 \times 10} = \frac{10}{30}$

1.14 Examples:
a. $\frac{21}{28} = \frac{21 \times 10}{28 \times 10} = \frac{210}{280}$
b. $\frac{21}{28} = \frac{21 \div 7}{28 \div 7} = \frac{3}{4}$

1.15 Examples:
a. $\frac{3}{5} = \frac{3 \times 10}{5 \times 10} = \frac{30}{50}$
b. $\frac{3}{5} = \frac{3 \times 5}{5 \times 5} = \frac{15}{25}$

1.16 Examples:
a. $\frac{100}{200} = \frac{100 \div 100}{200 \div 100} = \frac{1}{2}$
b. $\frac{100}{200} = \frac{100 \div 2}{200 \div 2} = \frac{50}{100}$

1.17 Examples:
a. $\frac{7}{12} = \frac{7 \times 100}{12 \times 100} = \frac{700}{1{,}200}$
b. $\frac{7}{12} = \frac{7 \times 2}{12 \times 2} = \frac{14}{24}$

1.18 Examples:
a. $\frac{6}{9} = \frac{6 \div 3}{9 \div 3} = \frac{2}{3}$
b. $\frac{6}{9} = \frac{6 \times 2}{9 \times 2} = \frac{12}{18}$

1.19 $\frac{7}{14} = \frac{7 \div 7}{14 \div 7} = \frac{1}{2}$

1.20 $\frac{6}{9} = \frac{6 \div 3}{9 \div 3} = \frac{2}{3}$

1.21 $\frac{3}{8}$

1.22 $\frac{20}{25} = \frac{20 \div 5}{25 \div 5} = \frac{4}{5}$

1.23 $\frac{1 + 2}{4} = \frac{3}{4}$

1.24 $\frac{3 - 2}{8} = \frac{1}{8}$

1.25 $\frac{6 + 3}{11} = \frac{9}{11}$

1.26 $\frac{4 - 3}{10} = \frac{1}{10}$

1.27 $\frac{8 - 3}{9} = \frac{5}{9}$

1.28 $\frac{7 + 3}{7} = \frac{10}{7}$

1.29 $\frac{14 + 6}{13} = \frac{20}{13}$

1.30 $\frac{6 - 1}{13} = \frac{5}{13}$

1.31 20

1.32 6

1.33 24

1.34 63

1.35 12

1.36 20

1.37 15

1.38 72

1.39 $\frac{1}{4} = \frac{1 \times 5}{4 \times 5} = \frac{5}{20}$

1.40 $\frac{1}{2} = \frac{1 \times 3}{2 \times 3} = \frac{3}{6}$

1.41 $\frac{3}{8} = \frac{3 \times 3}{8 \times 3} = \frac{9}{24}$

1.42 $\frac{4}{9} = \frac{4 \times 7}{9 \times 7} = \frac{28}{63}$

1.43 $\frac{1}{3} = \frac{1 \times 4}{3 \times 4} = \frac{4}{12}$

1.44 $\frac{1}{4} = \frac{1 \times 5}{4 \times 5} = \frac{5}{20}$

1.45 $\frac{6}{5} = \frac{6 \times 3}{5 \times 3} = \frac{18}{15}$

1.46 $\frac{3}{8} = \frac{3 \times 9}{8 \times 9} = \frac{27}{72}$

1.47 $\frac{5}{20} + \frac{12}{20} = \frac{17}{20}$

1.48 $\frac{3}{6} + \frac{5}{6} = \frac{8}{6} = \frac{4}{3}$

1.49 $\frac{9}{24} + \frac{10}{24} = \frac{19}{24}$

1.50 $\frac{54}{63} + \frac{28}{63} = \frac{82}{63}$

1.51 $\frac{4}{12} + \frac{9}{12} = \frac{13}{12}$

1.52 $\frac{5}{20} + \frac{6}{20} = \frac{11}{20}$

1.53 $\frac{18}{15} + \frac{15}{15} = \frac{33}{15} = \frac{11}{5}$

1.54 $\frac{27}{72} + \frac{8}{72} = \frac{35}{72}$

1.55 $\frac{12}{20} - \frac{5}{20} = \frac{7}{20}$

1.56 $\frac{5}{6} - \frac{3}{6} = \frac{2}{6} = \frac{1}{3}$

1.57 $\frac{10}{24} - \frac{9}{24} = \frac{1}{24}$

1.58 $\frac{54}{63} - \frac{28}{63} = \frac{26}{63}$

1.59 $\frac{9}{12} - \frac{4}{12} = \frac{5}{12}$

1.60 $\frac{6}{20} - \frac{5}{20} = \frac{1}{20}$

1.61 $\frac{18}{15} - \frac{15}{15} = \frac{3}{15} = \frac{1}{5}$

1.62 $\frac{27}{72} - \frac{8}{72} = \frac{19}{72}$

1.63 $2 + 4 = 6$; $\frac{2}{3} + \frac{1}{8} = \frac{16}{24} + \frac{3}{24} = \frac{19}{24}$; $6\frac{19}{24}$

1.64 $1 + 3 = 4$; $\frac{1}{9} + \frac{4}{5} = \frac{5}{45} + \frac{36}{45} = \frac{41}{45}$; $4\frac{41}{45}$

1.65 $3 + 2 = 5; \frac{3}{8} + \frac{1}{6} = \frac{9}{24} + \frac{4}{24} = \frac{13}{24}; 5\frac{13}{24}$

1.66 $5 - 3 = 2; \frac{5}{9} - \frac{1}{3} = \frac{5}{9} - \frac{3}{9} = \frac{2}{9}; 2\frac{2}{9}$

1.67 $2 - 1 = 1; \frac{4}{5} - \frac{1}{2} = \frac{8}{10} - \frac{5}{10} = \frac{3}{10}; 1\frac{3}{10}$

1.68 $4 - 2 = 2; \frac{5}{8} - \frac{1}{9} = \frac{45}{72} - \frac{8}{72} = \frac{37}{72}; 2\frac{37}{72}$

1.69 $\frac{13}{9} + \frac{10}{3} = \frac{13}{9} + \frac{30}{9} = \frac{43}{9}$

1.70 $\frac{13}{4} + \frac{13}{2} = \frac{13}{4} + \frac{26}{4} = \frac{39}{4}$

1.71 $\frac{1}{5} + \frac{7}{3} = \frac{3}{15} + \frac{35}{15} = \frac{38}{15}$

1.72 $\frac{19}{6} - \frac{3}{2} = \frac{19}{6} - \frac{9}{6} = \frac{10}{6} = \frac{5}{3}$

1.73 $\frac{11}{8} - \frac{3}{4} = \frac{11}{8} - \frac{6}{8} = \frac{5}{8}$

1.74 $\frac{9}{2} - \frac{21}{8} = \frac{36}{8} - \frac{21}{8} = \frac{15}{8}$

1.75 $\frac{3 \times 2}{4 \times 3} = \frac{6}{12} = \frac{1}{2}$

1.76 $\frac{1 \times 1}{8 \times 9} = \frac{1}{72}$

1.77 $\frac{3 \times 4}{7 \times 5} = \frac{12}{35}$

1.78 $\frac{1 \times 1}{2 \times 2} = \frac{1}{4}$

1.79 $\frac{5 \times 1}{6 \times 2} = \frac{5}{12}$

1.80 $\frac{8 \times 3}{7 \times 5} = \frac{24}{35}$

1.81 $\frac{7}{12} \times \frac{4}{3} = \frac{28}{36} = \frac{7}{9}$

1.82 $\frac{5}{8} \times \frac{5}{2} = \frac{25}{16}$

1.83 $\frac{4}{3} \times \frac{2}{1} = \frac{8}{3}$

1.84 $\frac{1}{6} \times \frac{5}{3} = \frac{5}{18}$

1.85 $\frac{6}{7} \times \frac{2}{3} = \frac{12}{21} = \frac{4}{7}$

1.86 $\frac{5}{2} \times \frac{11}{8} = \frac{55}{16}$

1.87 $\frac{5}{4} \div \frac{7}{1} = \frac{5}{4} \times \frac{1}{7} = \frac{5}{28}$

1.88 $\frac{23}{8} \div \frac{1}{4} = \frac{23}{8} \times \frac{4}{1} = \frac{92}{8} = \frac{23}{2}$

1.89 $\frac{18}{5} \div \frac{7}{3} = \frac{18}{5} \times \frac{3}{7} = \frac{54}{35}$

1.90 $\frac{13}{2} \div \frac{9}{8} = \frac{13}{2} \times \frac{8}{9} = \frac{104}{18} = \frac{52}{9}$

1.91 $\frac{14}{3} \div \frac{13}{8} = \frac{14}{3} \times \frac{8}{13} = \frac{112}{39}$

1.92 $\frac{3}{4} + \frac{7}{12} = \frac{9}{12} + \frac{7}{12} = \frac{16}{12} = \frac{4}{3}$ hours

1.93 $1\frac{2}{3} + 2\frac{1}{4} = \frac{5}{3} + \frac{9}{4} = \frac{20}{12} + \frac{27}{12} = \frac{47}{12}$ cups

1.94 $12\frac{1}{2} + 14\frac{3}{4} = \frac{25}{2} + \frac{59}{4} = \frac{50}{4} + \frac{59}{4} = \frac{109}{4}$ dozen

1.95 $12\frac{1}{2} + 36\frac{2}{3} = \frac{25}{2} + \frac{110}{3} = \frac{75}{6} + \frac{220}{6} = \frac{295}{6}$ yards

1.96 $\frac{1}{5} + \frac{3}{8} = \frac{8}{40} + \frac{15}{40} = \frac{23}{40}$ of the food

1.97 $3\frac{1}{2} - 1\frac{1}{6} = \frac{7}{2} - \frac{7}{6} = \frac{21}{6} - \frac{7}{6} = \frac{14}{6} =$
$\frac{7}{3}$ yards

1.98 $18\frac{1}{2} - 17\frac{3}{4} = \frac{37}{2} - \frac{71}{4} = \frac{74}{4} - \frac{71}{4} =$
$\frac{3}{4}$ gallon

1.99 $6\frac{1}{8} - 2\frac{1}{2} = \frac{49}{8} - \frac{5}{2} = \frac{49}{8} - \frac{20}{8} =$
$\frac{29}{8}$ cups

1.100 $36 \times 12\frac{3}{4} = \frac{36}{1} \times \frac{51}{4} = \frac{1,836}{4} =$
459 bushels

1.101 $5 \times \frac{1}{8} = \frac{5}{8}$ of the pie

1.102 $6\frac{1}{2} \times 7 = \frac{13}{2} \times \frac{7}{1} = \frac{91}{2}$ cents

1.103 $450 \times \frac{1}{2} = \frac{450}{2} = 225$ pounds

1.104 $\frac{1}{10} \times 600 = \frac{600}{10} = 60$ dollars

1.105 $1\frac{3}{4} \times 5 = \frac{7}{4} \times \frac{5}{1} = \frac{35}{4}$ miles

1.106 $\frac{3}{4} \times \frac{1}{2} = \frac{3}{8}$ quart

1.107 $6 \div 1\frac{3}{4} = 6 \div \frac{7}{4} = \frac{6}{1} \times \frac{4}{7} = \frac{24}{7}$ hours

1.108 $18 \div \frac{3}{4} = 18 \times \frac{4}{3} = \frac{72}{3} = 24$ pieces

1.109 $11\frac{1}{5} \div 7 = \frac{56}{5} \div \frac{7}{1} = \frac{56}{5} \times \frac{1}{7} =$
$\frac{56}{35} = \frac{8}{5}$ feet

1.110 $425 \div \frac{1}{2} = 425 \times \frac{2}{1} = 850$ plots

II. SECTION TWO

2.1 0.5

2.2 $0.\overline{3}$

2.3 0.75

2.4 0.6

2.5 $0.8\overline{3}$

2.6 0.143

2.7 0.875

2.8 0.4

2.9 0.6

2.10 0.15

2.11 $\frac{2}{10} = \frac{1}{5}$

2.12 $\frac{625}{1,000} = \frac{5}{8}$

2.13 $\frac{75}{100} = \frac{3}{4}$

2.14 $\frac{5}{10} = \frac{1}{2}$

2.15 $\frac{3}{100}$

2.16
$$\begin{array}{r} 3.14 \\ +\ 17.8 \\ \hline 20.94 \end{array}$$

2.17
$$\begin{array}{r} 7.610 \\ -\ 0.043 \\ \hline 7.567 \end{array}$$

```
2.18      142.3
        +    .07
        ---------
          142.37

2.19      5,387.1
        -    16.5
        ---------
          5,370.6

2.20      107.3
        +   0.8598
        ----------
          108.1598

2.21      3.100
        - 0.674
        -------
          2.426

2.22       3.7
        x 0.14
        ------
           148
           37
        ------
         0.518

2.23      14.8
        x  1.7
        ------
          1036
          148
        ------
          2.516

2.24       14.3
        x 0.017
        -------
           1001
           143
        -------
          0.2431

2.25      0.6421
        x    3.9
        --------
           57789
          19263
        --------
          2.50419

2.26      3,000

2.27      47.314

2.28      16,740

2.29      73,414.2

2.30      9,900,000
```

```
2.31      0.147

2.32      4.983

2.33      0.005734

2.34      0.004

               2.7872 = 2.787
2.35      47)131.0000
             94
             370
             329
              410
              376
               340
               329
                110
                 94

              81.8888 = 81.889
2.36      18)1474.0000
            144
              34
              18
              160
              144
               160
               144
                160
                144
                 160
                 144

            0.1684 = 0.168
2.37      38)6.4000
            38
            260
            228
             320
             304
              160
              152

                3.4063 = 3.406
2.38      411)1400.0000
              1233
               1670
               1644
                2600
                2466
                 1340
                 1233
```

2.39 1 kilogram = 1,000 grams;
1 gram = 0.001 kilogram =
0.002206 pounds

2.40
```
  2,034
    571.835
+     0.082
  2,605.917
```

2.41
```
  $ 2.85
x     67
    1995
   1710
 $190.95
```

2.42
```
              2.320 = $2.32
16,200)37,585.600
       32400
        51856
        48600
         32560
         32400
          1600
```

2.43
```
  $3,424.72
 - 2,147.31
  $1,277.41
```

2.44
```
   12.75
x   10.5
    6375
  1275
  133.875 sq. ft.
```

2.45
```
        120 miles
125)15,000
    125
     250
     250
       0
```

2.46
```
   2.342
 - 2.087
   0.255 inch
```

2.47
```
$  84.70
x     36
   50820
  25410
$3,049.20
```

2.48
```
   3.5
x  7.5
   175
  245
  26.25
```

2.49
```
   47.3
x   2.5
   2365
   946
  118.25 miles
```

2.50
```
   10,250
x   0.002
   20.500 = 20.5 inches
```

2.51
```
          89.6 mph
125)11200.0
     1000
      1200
      1125
        750
        750
          0
```

2.52 $1,234.70 (move the decimal point one place to the left)

2.53
```
     0.312 = $0.31
24)7.500
    72
     30
     24
      60
      48
```

III. SECTION THREE

3.1 0.67

3.2 0.03

3.3 1.47

3.4 0.004

3.5 1.384

3.6 0.14

3.7 43%

3.8 130%

3.9 1%

3.10 70%

3.11 65%

3.12 4%

3.13 0.06 x 124 = 7.44

3.14 1.03 x 19 = 19.57

3.15 0.421 x 375.4 = 158.0434

3.16 0.054 x 900 = 48.6

3.17 0.13 x 130 = 16.9

3.18 0.755 x 299.8 = 226.349

3.19 $0.8 = \frac{8}{10} = \frac{4}{5}$

3.20 $0.75 = \frac{75}{100} = \frac{3}{4}$

3.21 $0.875 = \frac{875}{1,000} = \frac{7}{8}$

3.22 $0.45 = \frac{45}{100} = \frac{9}{20}$

3.23 $0.02 = \frac{2}{100} = \frac{1}{50}$

3.24 $0.125 = \frac{125}{1,000} = \frac{1}{8}$

3.25 0.333 = 33.3%

3.26 0.9 = 90%

3.27 0.125 = 12.5%

3.28 0.6 = 60%

3.29 0.5 = 50%

3.30 0.143 = 14.3%

3.31 0.24 x 1,321 = 317.04

3.32 0.75 x 90 = 67.5

3.33 0.195 x 600 = 117

3.34 0.48 x 576 = 276.48

3.35 0.12 x 750 = 90

3.36 0.08 x 1,249 = 99.92

3.37 120 ÷ 371 = 0.323 = 32.3%

3.38 150 ÷ 200 = 0.75 = 75%

3.39 84 ÷ 212 = 0.396 = 39.6%

3.40 10 ÷ 85 = 0.118 = 11.8%

3.41 317 ÷ 142 = 2.232 = 223.2%

3.42 15 ÷ 1,500 = 0.01 = 1%

3.43 81 ÷ 0.10 = 810

3.44 100 ÷ 0.19 = 526.316

3.45 303 ÷ 0.93 = 325.806

3.46 130 ÷ 0.125 = 1,040

3.47 62 ÷ 1.12 = 55.357

3.48 50 ÷ 0.85 = 58.824

3.49 42 ÷ 0.12 = 350

3.50 300 ÷ 621 = 0.483 = 48.3%

3.51 43 ÷ 1.20 = $35.8\overline{3}$

3.52 0.165 x 4.371 = 721.215

3.53 0.81 x 403 = 326.43

3.54 99 ÷ 0.18 = 550

3.55 72 x 0.375 = 27 people

3.56 3 x 3.49 = 10.47 bushels

3.57 400 ÷ 640 = 0.625 = 62.5%

3.58 $200,000 x 2.50 = $500,000

3.59 $200,000 x 2.50 = $500,000
$500,000 + $200,000 = $700,000

3.60 $11,250 x 0.31 = $3,487.50

3.61 $227.50 ÷ 0.91 = $250

3.62 $70.00 ÷ $87.50 = 0.8 = 80%

CONSUMER MATHEMATICS 3
SOLUTION KEY

I. SECTION ONE

1.1 $16,000 ÷ 52 = $307.69

1.2 George is paid bi-weekly.
$14,500 ÷ 26 = $557.69

1.3 $15,000 ÷ 24 = $625.00

1.4 $27,000 ÷ 12 = $2,250.00

1.5 $1,200 x 12 = $14,400

1.6 $900 x 26 = $23,400

1.7 $650 x 52 = $33,800

1.8 $700 x 24 = $16,800

1.9
a. 40
b. 40 x $3.75 = $150

1.10
a. 30
b. 30 x $3.00 = $90

1.11
a. 38$\frac{3}{4}$
b. 38$\frac{3}{4}$ x $2.75 =
38.75 x $2.75 = $106.56

1.12
a. 50 - 40 = 10 overtime hours
50 + ($\frac{1}{2}$ x 10) = 50 + 5 = 55
b. 55 x $4.25 = $233.75

1.13
a. 47$\frac{1}{2}$ - 40 = 7$\frac{1}{2}$ overtime hours
47$\frac{1}{2}$ + ($\frac{1}{2}$ x 7$\frac{1}{2}$) = 47$\frac{1}{2}$ +
($\frac{1}{2}$ x $\frac{15}{2}$) = 47$\frac{1}{2}$ + $\frac{15}{4}$ = 51$\frac{1}{4}$
b. 51$\frac{1}{4}$ x $4.25 = 51.25 x
$4.25 = $217.81

1.14
a. 44 - 40 = 4 overtime hours
44 + ($\frac{1}{2}$ x 4) = 44 + 2 = 46
b. 46 x $4.25 = $195.50

1.15
a. 832
b. 832 x $0.10 = $83.20

1.16
a. 518
b. 518 x $0.17 = $88.06

1.17
a. 371
b. 371 x $0.35 = $129.85

1.18 0.30 x $750 = $225

1.19 0.10 x $1,043 = $104.30
$104.30 + $75.00 = $179.30

1.20 $37,500 - $43,000 = ($5,500)

1.21 $20,410 + $9,300 = $29,710
expenses
$43,750 - $29,710 = $14,040

1.22 $25,000 - $12,800 = $12,200

II. SECTION TWO

2.1 $8.70

2.2 $20.70

2.3 $37.10

2.4
a. $29.80
b. 0.02 x $196 = $3.92
c. 0.015 x $196 = $2.94
d. $29.80 + $3.92 + $2.94 =
$36.66

2.5
a. $8.00
b. 0.02 x $75 = $1.50
c. 0.015 x $75 = $1.13
d. $8.00 + $1.50 + $1.13 =
$10.63

2.6
a. $1.80
b. 0.02 x $67.50 = $1.35
c. 0.015 x $67.50 = $1.01
d. $1.80 + $1.35 + $1.01 =
$4.16

2.7
a. $15.70
b. 0.03 x $98 = $2.94
c. 0.0605 x $98 = $5.93
d. $15.70 + $2.94 + $5.93 =
$24.57
e. $98.00 - $24.57 = $73.43

2.8 a. $37.30
b. 0.03 x $240 = $7.20
c. 0.0605 x $240 = $14.52
d. $37.30 + $7.20 + $14.52 = $59.02
e. $240.00 - $59.02 = $180.98

2.9 a. $24.50
b. 0.03 x $150 = $4.50
c. 0.0605 x $150 = $9.08
d. $24.50 + $4.50 + $9.08 = $38.08
e. $150.00 - $38.08 = $111.92

2.10 Teacher check

2.11 49¢ x 0.07 = 3.43 = 3¢

2.12 $8.95 x 0.05 = 0.4475 = $0.45 or 45¢

2.13 $247.50 x 0.04 = $9.90

2.14 $\frac{2,560,000}{80,000,000} = 0.032 = 3.2\%$

2.15 $\frac{8,640,000}{240,000,000} = 0.036 = 3.6\%$

2.16 0.032 x $42,000 = $1,344

2.17 0.0135 x $8,500 = $114.75

III. SECTION THREE

3.1 Teacher check

3.2 $175.76 ÷ $1,116.00 = 0.157 = 15.7%

3.3 $350.84 ÷ $1,116.00 = 0.314 = 31.4%

3.4 $50.00 ÷ $1,116.00 = 0.045 = 4.5%

3.5 $30.00 ÷ $1,116.00 = 0.027 = 2.7%

3.6 $35.00 ÷ $1,116.00 = 0.031 = 3.1%

3.7 $200.00 ÷ $1,116.00 = 0.179 = 17.9%

3.8 $106.40 ÷ $1,116.00 = 0.095 = 9.5%

3.9 $168.00 ÷ $1,116.00 = 0.151 = 15.1%

3.10 $8 ÷ $75 = 0.107 = 10.7%

3.11 $18 ÷ $75 = 0.24 = 24%

3.12 $15 ÷ $75 = 0.2 = 20%

3.13 $12 ÷ $75 = 0.16 = 16%

3.14 $15 ÷ $75 = 0.2 = 20%

3.15 $7 ÷ $75 = 0.093 = 9.3%

3.16 0.11 x $18,600 = $2,046

3.17 0.15 x $18,600 = $2,790

3.18 0.10 x $18,600 = $1,860

3.19 0.20 x $18,600 = $3,720

3.20 0.12 x $18,600 = $2,232

3.21 0.09 x $18,600 = $1,674

3.22 0.13 x $18,600 = $2,418

3.23 0.10 x $18,600 = $1,860

3.24 0.10 x $9,742.41 = $974.24

3.25 0.129 x $9,742.41 = $1,256.77

3.26 0.274 x $9,742.41 = $2,669.42

3.27 0.162 x $9,742.41 = $1,578.27

3.28 0.089 x $9,742.41 = $867.07

3.29 0.118 x $9,742.41 = $1,149.60

3.30 0.074 x $9,742.41 = $720.94

3.31 0.044 x $9,742.41 = $428.67

3.32 0.01 x $9,742.41 = $ 97.42

3.33 Teacher check

3.34 Any order:
a. Tithe first.
b. Let God lead.
c. Determine fixed expenses.
d. Estimate other expenses.
e. Plan a realistic budget.
f. Divide your paycheck up by the budget.
g. Do not spend money you do not have.

IV. SECTION FOUR

4.1 $125.39 + $76.00 - $201.39

4.2 $10.50 + $9.00 = $19.50

4.3 10¢ + 29¢ = 39¢

4.4 $0.98 - $0.67 = $0.31

4.5 $30.00 ÷ 12 = $2.50 each
$5 - $2.50 = $2.50

4.6 $16.00 - $12.95 = $3.05

4.7 $15.76 - $8.00 = $7.76

4.8 $300.00 - $75.38 = $224.62

4.9 $89.95 - $35.00 = $54.95

4.10 M = 0.40 x $75.00 = $30.00
S = $75.00 + $30.00 = $105.00

4.11 M = 0.50 x $120.00 = $60.00
S = $120.00 + $60.00 = $180.00

4.12 M = 0.30 x $98.00 = $29.40
S = $98.00 - $29.40 = $68.60

4.13 M = 0.11 x $2.19 = $0.24
S = $2.19 - $0.24 = $1.95

4.14 a. $198.99 - $120.37 = $78.62
b. $78.62 ÷ $120.37 = 0.653 = 65.3%
c. $78.62 ÷ $198.99 = 0.395 = 39.5%

4.15 a. $0.43 + $0.43 = $0.86
b. $0.43 ÷ $0.43 = 1 = 100%
c. $0.43 ÷ $0.86 = 0.5 = 50%

4.16 a. $1,000.00 - $427.41 = $572.59
b. $427.41 ÷ $572.59 = 0.746 = 74.6%
c. $427.41 ÷ $1,000.00 = 0.427 = 42.7%

4.17 Note: Figure (b) first.
a. $67.50 - $10.13 = $57.37
b. 0.15 x $67.50 = $10.13
c. $10.13 ÷ $57.37 = 0.177 = 17.7%

4.18 a. 0.50 x $19.00 = $9.50
b. $19.00 + $9.50 = $28.50
c. $9.50 ÷ $28.50 = 0.333 = 33.3%

4.19 0.02 x $38.95 = $0.78 discount
$38.95 - $0.78 = $38.17

4.20 $43.95 x 4 = $175.80
0.035 x $175.80 = $6.15 discount
$175.80 - $6.15 = $169.65

4.21 $1.10 x 19 = $20.90
$20.90 x 0.015 = $0.31
$20.90 - $0.31 = $20.59

4.22 $104.89 x 0.02 = $2.10
$104.89 - $2.10 = $102.79

4.23 $29.69 - $8.00 = $21.69

4.24 0.31 x $2.89 = $0.90
$2.89 - $0.90 = $1.99

4.25 0.50 x $53.98 = $26.99
$53.98 - $26.99 = $26.99

4.26 Hallcraft Holiday is in excellent condition. Three bedrooms, two bathrooms, dining room, and family room. Good landscaping, pool, covered patio, and garage.
7 rooms

4.27 Low cash to mortgage.
Two bedrooms, one bathroom.
No qualifying. Low monthly payments.
4 rooms

4.28 By owner. Three bedroom home, family room, fireplace, den, large master bedroom.
7 rooms

4.29 Four bedrooms, $1\frac{3}{4}$ bathrooms, family room, fireplace, pool, family-dining room, cement block fence, 2-car garage, between $50,000 and $60,000.
8 rooms

4.30 Three bedrooms, $1\frac{3}{4}$ bathrooms, fireplace, pool, upgraded carpet, custom drapes.
5 rooms

4.31 Teacher check

4.32 a (10¢ off a 58¢ can is 48¢ a can, which is more than 43¢ a can)

4.33 b (with this offer you are buying two loaves for 68¢, or 34¢ a loaf; this price is more economical than 53¢ a loaf)

4.34 b (30¢ off 74¢ is 44¢ a pound, which is less than 87¢ a pound)

4.35
a. 55¢ ÷ 46 = 1.2¢
b. 6 x 10 oz. = 60 oz.
75¢ ÷ 60 = 1.25¢
c. a

4.36
a. 59¢ ÷ 10 = 5.9¢
b. $1.53 ÷ 24 = 6.4¢
c. a

4.37
a. 2 lb. = 32 oz.
$1.69 ÷ 32 = 5.3¢
b. $0.59 ÷ 6 = 9.8¢
c. a

4.38
a. $1\frac{1}{2}$ lb. = 24 oz.
63¢ ÷ 24 = 2.6¢
b. 1 lb. = 16 oz.
39¢ ÷ 16 = 2.4¢
c. b

4.39
a. 89¢ ÷ 16 = 5.6¢
b. 59¢ ÷ 12 = 4.9¢
c. b

4.40
a. $146 x 36 = $5,256
b. $5,256 - $4,000 = $1,256
c. $4,000 ÷ $146 = 27.4 = 28

4.41
a. $143 x 15 = $2,145
b. $2,145 - $1,998 = $147
c. $1,998 ÷ $143 = 14

4.42
a. $11.00 x 24 = $264
$264 + $8.50 = $272.50
b. $272.50 - $200 = $72.50
c. $200 ÷ $11 = 18.2 = 19

CONSUMER MATHEMATICS 4
SOLUTION KEY

I. SECTION ONE

1.1 $28.23 x 30 = $846.90

1.2 Find the premium for a person aged 24 (27 - 3 = 24) under the "20-year Endowment" column: $42.34.
$42.34 x 25 = $1,058.50

1.3 $4.15 x 7 = $29.05

1.4 $34.55 x 50 = $1,727.50

1.5 a. 41 - 3 = 38
b. $20.04 x 30 = $601.20

1.6 a. 27 (he is closer to 27 than to 26)
b. $4.41 x 15 = $66.15

1.7 a. 0.51 x $846.90 = $431.92
b. 0.26 x $846.90 = $220.19
c. 0.09 x $846.90 = $76.22

1.8 a. 0.51 x $601.20 = $306.61
b. 0.26 x $601.20 = $156.31
c. 0.09 x $601.20 = $54.11

1.9 annual premium = $1,058.50
semi-annual premium =
0.51 x $1,058.50 = $539.84
yearly output for semi-annual premiums = 2 x $539.84 = $1,079.68
difference = $1,079.68 - $1,058.50 = $21.18

1.10 annual premium = $29.05
quarterly premium =
0.26 x $29.05 = $7.55
yearly output for quarterly premiums = 4 x $7.55 = $30.20
difference = $30.20 - $29.05 = $1.15

1.11 annual premium = $1,727.50
monthly premium =
0.09 x $1,727.50 = $155.48
yearly output for monthly premiums = 12 x $155.48 = $1,865.76
difference = $1,865.76 - $1,727.50 = $138.26

1.12 a. $10,000
b. $8,000
c. $18,000

1.13 $40,000

1.14 The man belongs to Class 2B.
a. $761.00 + $163.80 = $924.80
b. $976.96 + $196.60 = $1,173.56
c. $1,173.56 - $924.80 = $248.76

1.15 The family's car belongs to Class 1A.
a. $383.60 + $67.00 = $450.60
b. The car now belongs to Class 2A.
$709.30 + $124.80 = $834.10
c. $834.10 - $450.60 = $383.50

1.16 The company car belongs to Class 3.
$549.70 + $98.20 = $647.90

1.17 The Moser's car belongs to Class 2A.
$709.30 + $124.80 = $834.10

1.18 $298

1.19 $104

1.20 $52

1.21 Since Sam has a $100-deductible clause the insurance company pays $1,400 - $100 = $1,300 of the car repair expense. The insurance company also pays $500 for medical expenses, for a total of $1,300 + $500 = $1,800.

1.22 Since Glenda has a $50-deductible clause the insurance company will pay $350 - $50 = $300 of the car repair expense. The insurance company will also pay all of the hospital bill since $276 is less than the $2,000 coverage. The total amount that will be paid by the insurance company is $300 + $276 = $576.

1.23 $20

1.24 $84

1.25 $26

1.26 0.90 x $613.50 = $552.15

1.27 $417.25 - $32 = $385.25
$385.25 x 1.50 = $577.88
$577.88 + $32 = $609.88

1.28 $587.00 + $124.80 = $711.80 premium
2.50 x $711.80 = $1,779.50

1.29 d

1.30 f

1.31 c

1.32 h

1.33 b

1.34 e

1.35 a

1.36 false

1.37 true

1.38 true

1.39 false

1.40 true

1.41 Teacher check

II. SECTION TWO

2.1

CB
CITY BANK
MAIN AND CENTRAL OFFICE
PHOENIX, ARIZONA

1456
2-631/710

Date 2

PAY TO THE ORDER OF Grand Avenue Food Market $ 37.50

Thirty-seven and 50/100 DOLLARS

MEMO

Your Name

⑆710⑆0631⑆ 0631 9088 0000003750

2.2

CB
CITY BANK
MAIN AND CENTRAL OFFICE
PHOENIX, ARIZONA

1457
2-631/710

Date 2

PAY TO THE ORDER OF Glendale Community Church $ 47.98

Forty-seven and 98/100 DOLLARS

MEMO tithe

Your Name

⑆710⑆0631⑆ 0631 9088 0000004798

2.3

CHECK NO	DATE	CHECKS ISSUED TO OR DESCRIPTION OF DEPOSIT	AMOUNT OF CHECK	AMOUNT OF DEPOSIT	BALANCE FORWARD 358.27
3427		To Adams Meat Market For food	23.42		Check or Dep 23.42 Bal 334.85
3428		To West High School For Books & Supplies	14.95		Check or Dep 14.95 Bal 319.90
		To DEPOSIT For PAYCHECK		276.50	Check or Dep 276.50 Bal 596.40
3429		To Saguaro Mort Co. For house payment	219.93		Check or Dep 219.93 Bal 376.47
3430		To Alamo Power & Light For elect.	76.84		Check or Dep 76.84 Bal 299.63
		To For			Check or Dep Bal

2.4 Add the outstanding checks:
$25.00 + $75.21 + $117.84 = $218.05
Subtract from the ending balance:
$637.89 - $218.05 = $419.84
Add the deposit:
$419.84 + $216.00 = $635.84
Subtract the service charge from the balance in the record book:
$640.03 - $4.19 = $635.84
No, an error does not exist.

2.5 Add the outstanding checks:
$200.00 + $7.16 = $207.16
Subtract from the ending balance:
$1,227.75 - $207.16 = $1,020.59
Yes, an error exists.

2.6
a. Locate and add the amounts of outstanding checks.
b. Subtract outstanding check total from bank's ending balance.
c. Add to bank's record any deposits not yet credited.
d. Subtract from your record book any charges not yet recorded.
e. Compare the totals from the third and fourth steps; they should agree.

2.7 $800 x 0.035 x 7 = $196

2.8 $\$1,600 \times 0.06 = \frac{180}{360}$
$1,600 x 0.06 x 0.5 = $48

2.9 $100 x 0.08 x 20 = $160

2.10 $4,500 x 0.05 x 3 = $675

2.11 $\$10,000 \times 0.095 \times \frac{90}{360} =$
$10,000 x 0.095 x 0.25 = $237.50

2.12 $\$295 \times 0.07 \times \frac{270}{360} =$
$295 x 0.07 x 0.75 = $15.49

2.13 $500 x 0.048 x 5 = $120

2.14 $3,000 x 0.10 x 1 = $300

2.15
a. Find in the chart the amount of $1.00 at 8% for 14 years and multiply by $650:
2.9371936 x 650 = $1,909.18
b. $1,909.18 - $650 = $1,259.18

2.16
a. Find in the chart the amount of $1.00 at 6% for 25 years and multiply by $1,050:
4.2918707 x $1,050 = $4,506.46
b. $4,506.46 - $1,050 = $3,456.46

2.17
a. Find in the chart the amount of $1.00 at 3% for 10 years and multiply by $5,000:
1.3439164 x $5,000 = $6,719.58
b. $6,719.58 - $5,000 = $1,719.58

2.18
a. Find in the chart the amount of $1.00 at 4% for 5 years and multiply by $500:
1.2166529 x 500 = $608.33
b. $608.33 - $500 = $108.33

2.19
a. Find in the chart the amount of $1.00 at 1.5% for 3 years and multiply by $2,900:
1.0456784 x $2,900 = $3,032.47
b. $3,032.47 - $2,900 = $132.47

2.20
a. Find in the chart the amount of $1.00 at 2% for 9 years and multiply by $850:
1.1950926 x $850 = $1,015.83
b. $1,015.83 - $850 = $165.83

2.21 a. Find in the chart the amount of $1.00 at 8% for 5 years and multiply by $3,000:
1.4693281 x $3,000 = $4,407.98
b. $4,407.98 - $3,000 = $1,407.98
c. Find in the chart the amount of $1.00 at 4% for 10 years and multiply by $3,000:
1.4802443 x $3,000 = $4,440.73
d. $4,440.73 - $3,000 = $1,440.73
e. Find in the chart the amount of $1.00 at 2% for 20 years and multiply by $3,000:
1.4859474 x $3,000 = $4,457.84
f. $4,457.84 - $3,000 = $1,457.84

2.22 a. Find in the chart the amount of $1.00 at 6% for 10 years and multiply by $900:
1.7908477 x $900 = $1,611.76
b. $1,611.76 - $900 = $711.76
c. Find in the chart the amount of $1.00 at 3% for 20 years and multiply by $900:
1.8061112 x $900 = $1,625.50
d. $1,625.50 - $900 = $725.50
e. Find in the chart the amount of $1.00 at 1½% for 40 years and multiply by $900:
1.8140184 x $900 = $1,632.62
f. $1,632.62 - $900 = $732.62

2.23 a. Find in the chart the amount of $1.00 at 8% for 2 years and multiply by $5,000:
1.1664000 x $5,000 = $5,832.00
b. $5,832.00 - $5,000 = $832.00
c. Find in the chart the amount of $1.00 at 4% for 4 years and multiply by $5,000:
1.1698586 x $5,000 = $5,849.29
d. $5,849.29 - $5,000 = $849.29
e. Find in the chart the amount of $1.00 at 2% for 8 years and multiply by $5,000:
1.1716594 x $5,000 = $5,858.30
f. $5,858.30 - $5,000 = $858.30

2.24 a. Find in the chart the amount of $1.00 at 6% for 25 years and multiply by $1,500:
4.2918707 x $1,500 = $6,437.81
b. $6,437.81 - $1,500 = $4,937.81
c. Find in the chart the amount of $1.00 at 3% for 50 years and multiply by $1,500:
4.3839060 x $1,500 = $6,575.86
d. $6,575.86 - $1,500 = $5,075.86
e. Find in the chart the amount of $1.00 at 1½% for 100 years and multiply by $1,500:
4.4320457 x $1,500 = $6,648.07
f. $6,648.07 - $1,500 = $5,148.07

2.25 $250 x 0.11 x 2 = $55

2.26 $\$1{,}400 \times 0.09 \times \frac{270}{360} =$
$1,400 x 0.09 x 0.75 = $94.50

2.27 $5,000 x 0.11 x 3 = $1,650

2.28 $\$700 \times 0.105 \times \frac{90}{360} =$
$700 x 0.105 x 0.25 = $18.38

2.29 $1,090 x 0.08 x 5 = $436

2.30 false

2.31 true

2.32 true

2.33 false

2.34 false

2.35 c

2.36 f

2.37 d

2.38 a

2.39 b

III. SECTION THREE

3.1 a. $120,000 ÷ 40,000 = $3.00
b. $3.00 x 45 = $135.00

3.2 a. $50,000 ÷ 100,000 = $0.50
b. $0.50 x 25 = $12.50

3.3 a. $37,500 ÷ 50,000 = $0.75
b. $0.75 x 75 = $56.25

3.4 a. $109,600 ÷ 80,000 = $1.37
b. $6.85 ÷ $1.37 = 5

3.5 a. $1.00 x 75,000 = $75,000
b. $50.00 ÷ $1.00 = 50

3.6 Teacher check

3.7 Teacher check

CONSUMER MATHEMATICS 5
SOLUTION KEY

I. SECTION ONE

1.1 $\frac{1}{10} = 10^{-1}$
1 decimeter, 1 dm

1.2 $100 = 10^2$
1 hectoliter, 1 hl

1.3 $\frac{1}{1{,}000{,}000} = 10^{-6}$
1 microgram, 1 μg

1.4 $1{,}000 = 10^3$
1 kilosecond, 1 ks

1.5 $1{,}000{,}000 = 10^6$
1 mega-ampere, 1 Ma

1.6 1 gigacandela, 1 Gcd

1.7 $10{,}000 = 10^4 = 10 \times 10^3$
10 kilograms, 10 kg

1.8 $\frac{1}{500{,}000} = \frac{2}{2} \times \frac{1}{500{,}000}$
$= \frac{2}{1{,}000{,}000} = \frac{2}{10^6} = 2 \times 10^{-6}$
= 2 microliters, 2 μl

1.9 1 nanosecond = 10^{-9} of a second = 0.000000001 second = 1-billionth second

1.10 1 hectometer = 10^2 meters = 100 meters

1.11 1 milliampere = 10^{-3} of an ampere = 1 thousandth ampere

1.12 1 megaton = 10^6 tons = 1 million tons

1.13 $10\frac{1}{2} \times 25.4 =$
$10.5 \times 25.4 =$
266.7 mm

1.14 $18 \times \frac{1}{1.609} =$
$18 \times 0.6215 =$
11.2 mi.

1.15 $100 \times 9.144 \times 10^{-1} =$
$100 \times 0.9144 =$
91.4 m

1.16 $600 \times 1.609 = 965.4$ km/hr.

1.17 b

1.18 c
$\frac{1}{2.54 \times 10^{-2}} = \frac{1}{0.0254} = 39.4$

1.19 a
Dividing 100 by 1.609 is the same as multiplying 100 by $\frac{1}{1.609}$.

1.20 $125 \times 8.36 \times 10^{-1} =$
$125 \times 0.836 =$
104.5 m^2

1.21 $9\frac{1}{2} \times \frac{1}{6.45} =$
$9.5 \times 0.155 =$
1.47 $in.^2$

1.22 $16 \times \frac{1}{4.05 \times 10^{-3}} =$
$16 \times \frac{1}{0.00405} =$
$16 \times 246.914 =$
3,950.6 acres

1.23 $50 \times 259 = 12{,}950$ hectares

1.24 true;
$5 \times \frac{1}{8.36 \times 10^{-1}} =$
$5 \times \frac{1}{0.836} = 5 \times 1.196$

1.25 false

1.26 true

1.27 true

1.28 $25 \times 4.732 \times 10^{-1} =$
$25 \times 0.4732 = 11.83$ l

1.29 $1 \times 946.36 = 946.36\ \text{cm}^3$

1.30 $6 \times \frac{1}{29.574} =$

$\frac{6}{29.574} = 0.203$ fluid oz.

1.31 $4 \times 1.164 \times 9.463 \times 10^{-1} =$
$4 \times 1.164 \times 0.9463 =$
4.406 liters

1.32 e

$10 \times \frac{1}{3.785} = \frac{10}{3.785} = 2.64$ gallons

1.33 a
$5 \times 2.832 \times 10^{-2} =$
$5 \times 0.02832 = 0.14$ cubic meters

1.34 b
$7 \times 7.645 \times 10^{-1} =$
$7 \times 0.7645 = 5.35$ cubic meters

1.35 d

$3 \times \frac{1}{4.732 \times 10^{-1}} =$

$3 \times \frac{1}{0.4732} =$

$\frac{3}{0.4732} = 6.34$ pints

1.36 $15 \times 9.072 \times 10^{-1} =$
$15 \times 0.9072 =$
13.608 or 13.61 metric tons

1.37 $150 \times 64.798 = 9{,}719.7$ mg

1.38 $100 \times \frac{1}{4.536 \times 10^{-1}} =$

$100 \times \frac{1}{0.4536} =$

$\frac{100}{0.4536} = 220.46$ lb.

1.39 $65 \times 4.536 \times 10^{-1} =$
$65 \times 0.4536 = 29.48$ kg

1.40 $°\text{C} = (96 - 32) \times \frac{5}{9}$
$= 64 \times \frac{5}{9}$
$= \frac{320}{9}$
$= 35.6°\text{C}$

1.41 $°\text{F} = \frac{9}{5} \times 10 + 32$
$= 18 + 32$
$= 50°\text{F}$

1.42 $°\text{F} = \frac{9}{5} \times 2 + 32$
$= \frac{18}{5} + 32$
$= 3.6 + 32$
$= 35.6°\text{F}$

II. SECTION TWO

2.1 $A = \frac{1}{2}(16.5\ \text{in.})(7.5\ \text{in.})$
$A = \frac{1}{2}(123.75\ \text{in.}^2)$
$A = 61.875\ \text{in.}^2$

2.2 $A = \frac{1}{2}(13\ \text{cm})(4\ \text{cm})$
$A = \frac{1}{2}(52\ \text{cm}^2)$
$A = 26\ \text{cm}^2$

2.3 $A = \frac{1}{2}(20\ \text{in.})(4\ \text{in.})$
$A = \frac{1}{2}(80\ \text{in.}^2)$
$A = 40\ \text{in.}^2$
$A = 40 \times 6.45$
$A = 258\ \text{cm}^2$

2.4

10 ft. 10 ft.
h
8 ft. 8 ft.

$8^2 + h^2 = 10^2$
$h^2 = 10^2 - 8^2$
$h^2 = 100 - 64$
$h^2 = 36$
$\sqrt{h^2} = \sqrt{36}$
$h = 6$ ft.

$a^2 + b^2 = c^2$
$a = \frac{\text{base}}{2}$
b = height
c = side

2.4 cont.

$A = \frac{1}{2}(16 \text{ ft.})(6 \text{ ft.})$
$A = \frac{1}{2}(96 \text{ ft.}^2)$
$A = 48 \text{ ft.}^2$

2.5 $A = a \times b$
$A = 15 \times 19.5$
$A = 292.5 \text{ cm}^2$

2.6 $A = a \times b$
$A = 12 \text{ ft.} \times 12 \text{ ft.}$
$A = 144 \text{ ft.}^2$
$A = 144 \times 9.29 \times 10^{-2}$
$A = 144 \times 0.0929$
$A = 13.3776$ or 13.38 m^2

2.7 $A = a \times b$
$A = 16 \text{ cm} \times 22 \text{ cm}$
$A = 352 \text{ cm}^2$
$A = 352 \times \frac{1}{6.45}$
$A = \frac{352}{6.45}$
$A = 54.57 \text{ in.}^2$

2.8 false

2.9 false
$A = \frac{1}{2}bh$
$40 = \frac{1}{2}b(8)$
$40 = 4b$
$\frac{40}{4} = b$
$b = 10 \text{ cm}$

2.10 d
$A = a \times b$
$150 = 25 \times b$
$\frac{150}{25} = b$
$b = 6 \text{ m}$

2.11 a
$A = a \times a$
$A = 6 \text{ in.} \times 6 \text{ in.}$
$A = 36 \text{ in.}^2$
$A = 36 \times 6.45$
$A = 232.2$
$A = 232 \text{ cm}^2$

2.12 $A = \frac{1}{2}(a + b)h$
$A = \frac{1}{2}(12 + 16)(9)$
$A = \frac{1}{2}(28)(9)$
$A = (14)(9)$
$A = 126 \text{ cm}^2$

2.13 b
$A = \frac{1}{2}(a + b)h$
$A = \frac{1}{2}(5 + 8)14$
$A = \frac{1}{2}(13)(14)$
$A = 91 \text{ cm}^2$

2.14 $A = \pi r^2$
$A = 3.14(4.5)^2$
$A = 3.14(20.25)$
$A = 63.585$ or 63.59 cm^2

2.15 $A = \frac{1}{4}\pi d^2$
$A = \frac{1}{4}(3.14)(15)^2$
$A = \frac{1}{4}(3.14)(225)$
$A = 176.625$ or 176.63 in.^2

2.16 $C = 2\pi r$
$280 = 2(3.14)r$
$280 = 6.28r$
$\frac{280}{6.28} = r$
$r = 44.586$

$A = \pi r^2$
$A = 3.14\ (44.586)^2$
$A = 3.14\ (1987.9114)$
$A = 6{,}242 \text{ cm}^2$

2.17 $A = \pi r^2$
$A = 3.14(10)^2$
$A = 3.14(100)$
$A = 3\ 14 \text{ cm}^2$

2.18 $A = \pi r^2$
$A = 3.14(5)^2$
$A = 3.14(25)$
$A = 78.5 \text{ yd.}^2$
$A = 78.5 \times 8.36 \times 10^{-1}$
$A = 78.5 \times 0.836$
$A = 65.626$ or 65.63 m^2

2.19 $A = \pi ab$
$A = 3.14(4)(7)$
$A = 3.14(28)$
$A = 87.92$ or 88 in.^{2}
$A = 88 \times 6.45$
$A = 567.6$ cm^2

2.20 $a = 5$ cm; $b = 10$ cm

$A = \pi ab$
$A = 3.14(5)(10)$
$A = 3.14(50)$
$A = 157$ cm^2

2.21 $a = 4$ cm; $b = 7$ cm

$A = \pi ab$
$A = 3.14(4)(7)$
$A = 3.14(28)$
$A = 87.92$ or 88 cm^2

2.22 A(each tile) = 25 x 25 = 625 cm^2
A(kitchen) = $10\frac{1}{2}$ x 18 = 189 ft.^{2}

189 ft.^{2} = 189 x 144 = 27,216 in.^{2}

27,216 in.^{2} = 27,216 x 6.45 = 175,543.2 cm^2

Number of tiles needed =
$\frac{175,543.2}{625}$ = 280.87 or 281 tiles

2.23 A (bricks) = $8\frac{1}{2}$ x $3\frac{1}{2}$ x 400
= 8.5 x 3.5 x 400
= 11,900 in.^{2}
= $\frac{11,900}{144}$ ft.^{2}
= 82.64 ft.^{2}

A (wall) = length x height
82.64 = length x 4.5
$\frac{82.64}{4.5}$ = length
length = 18.36 or 18.4 ft.

2.24 diameter = 3' 4" + 1" + 1" = 3' 6" or 3.5'

$A = \frac{1}{4}\pi d^2$
$A = \frac{1}{4}(3.14)(3.5)^2$
$A = \frac{1}{4}(3.14)(12.25)$
$A = 9.6$ ft.^{2}

2.25 A (panel board) = 4 x 8 = 32 ft.^{2}

A (room) = 4 x $\frac{1}{2}$ x 8 x 12
= 192 ft.^{2}

Number of panels needed =
$\frac{192}{32}$ = 6 panels

2.26 A (each end and side panel) = 6' x 2' 6" = 6' x 2.5' = 15 ft.^{2}

A (end of shed) = 6 x 7.5 = 45 ft.^{2}

A (2 sides of shed) = 2 x 6 x 10 = 120 ft.^{2}

Total A (end and sides) = 45 + 120 = 165 ft.^{2}

Number of panels needed =
$\frac{165}{15}$ = 11 panels

2.27 A (each roof panel) = 4' 1" x 2' $6\frac{1}{2}$" = 49" x 30.5 = 1,494.5 in.^{2}

A (roof) = 2 x 10' x 4' $\frac{1}{2}$" = 2 x 120" x 48.5" = 11,640 in.^{2}

Number of panels needed =
$\frac{11,640}{1,494.5}$ = 7.8 or 8 panels

2.28 A = 2 x 10 x 6 = 120 ft.^{2}

2.29 A (end) = 6 x 7.5 = 45 ft.^{2}

A (gables) = 2 x $\frac{1}{2}$(7.5)(1.5) = 11.25 ft.^{2}

Total A (end and gables) = 45 + 11.25 = 56.25 ft.^{2}

2.30 A (roof) $= 2 \times 10' \times 4'\ \tfrac{1}{2}"$
$= 2 \times 120" \times 48.5"$
$= 11{,}640$ in.^{2}
$= \dfrac{11{,}640}{144}$ ft.^{2}
$= 80.8$ ft.^{2}

2.31 A (end) $= 45$ ft.^{2}
A (sides) $= 120$ ft.^{2}
A (roof) $= 80.8$ ft.^{2}
A (gables) $= 11.25$ ft.^{2}
Total $A = 257.05$ ft.^{2}

2.32 $A = 16 \times 14 = 224$ in.^{2}

2.33 $12'\ 6" \div 2\tfrac{1}{2}" =$
$150" \div 2.5" = 60$ bricks

2.34 $16 \div 8 = 2$ bricks long
$14 \div 3\tfrac{1}{2} = 4$ bricks wide
$2 \times 4 = 8$ bricks

2.35 $12'\ 6" \div 2\tfrac{1}{2} =$
$150" \div 2.5" = 60$ rows

2.36 8 bricks x 60 rows = 480 bricks
2 x 480 = 960 bricks

2.37 A (2 sides) $= 2 \times 12'\ 6" \times 16"$
$= 2 \times 150" \times 16"$
$= 4{,}800$ in.^{2}
A (2 sides) $= 2 \times 12'\ 6" \times 14"$
$= 2 \times 150" \times 14"$
$= 4{,}200$ in.^{2}
A (top and bottom) $= 2 \times 16" \times 14"$
$= 448$ in.^{2}
Total $A = 4{,}800 + 4{,}200 + 448$
$= 9{,}448$ in.^{2}
$= \dfrac{9{,}448}{144}$ ft.^{2}
$= 65.6$ ft.^{2}

III. SECTION THREE

3.1

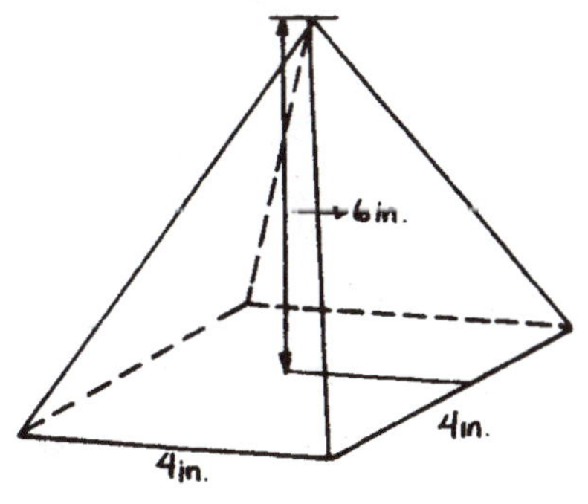

3.1 cont.

$V = \tfrac{1}{3}(4 \times 4)(6)$
$V = \tfrac{1}{3}(16)(6)$
$V = 32$ in.^{3}

3.2 $A = 2(4 \times 6 + 4 \times 8 + 6 \times 8)$
$A = 2(24 + 32 + 48)$
$A = 2(104)$
$A = 208$ cm^2

3.3 $A = 6a^2$
$96 = 6a^2$
$\dfrac{96}{6} = a^2$
$a^2 = 16$
$\sqrt{a^2} = \sqrt{16}$
$a = 4$ in.

3.4

5
5
$2.5\sqrt{3}$ m
5
5
5
5 m

$A = \tfrac{1}{2}(15)(2.5\sqrt{3})$
$A = 32.48$ m^2

3.5 $V = (15)(12)(9)$
$V = 1{,}620$ in.^{3}

3.6

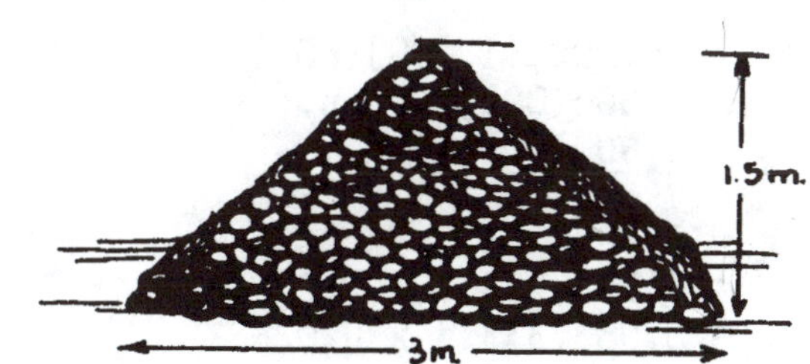

3.6 cont.

$$1.5^2 + h^2 = 3^2$$
$$h^2 = 3^2 - 1.5^2$$
$$h^2 = 9 - 2.25$$
$$h^2 = 6.75$$
$$\sqrt{h^2} = \sqrt{6.75}$$
$$h = 2.6 \text{ m}$$

$$A \text{ (base)} = \tfrac{1}{2}bh$$
$$= \tfrac{1}{2}(3)(2.6)$$
$$= 3.9 \text{ m}^2$$

$$V = \tfrac{1}{3}(3.9)(1.5) = 1.95 \text{ m}^3$$

3.7 $A = 2(4.5 \times 6.8 + 4.5 \times 8.2 + 6.8 \times 8.2)$
$$A = 2(30.6 + 36.9 + 55.76)$$
$$A = 2(123.26)$$
$$A = 246.52 \text{ cm}^2$$

3.8 $A \text{ (base)} = \pi r^2$
$$= 3.14(3.5)^2$$
$$= 3.14\ (12.25)$$
$$= 38.465 \text{ in.}^2$$

$$V = \tfrac{1}{3}(38.465)(6.5)$$
$$V = 83.34 \text{ in.}^3$$
$$V = \frac{83.34}{1{,}728} \text{ ft.}^3$$
$$V = 0.048229 \text{ or } 0.048 \text{ ft.}^3$$
$$V = 0.048 \times 2.832 \times 10^{-2}$$
$$V = 0.048 \times 0.02832$$
$$V = 0.00136 \text{ m}^3$$

3.9 300 cubits = 300(20) = 6,000 in.
50 cubits = 50(20) = 1,000 in.
30 cubits = 30(20) = 600 in.

$$V = (6{,}000)(1{,}000)(600)$$
$$V = 3{,}600{,}000{,}000 \text{ in.}^3$$
$$V = \frac{3{,}600{,}000{,}000}{1{,}728} \text{ ft.}^3$$
$$V = 2{,}083{,}333.3 \text{ ft.}^3$$
$$V = 2{,}083{,}333.3 \times 2.832 \times 10^{-2}$$
$$V = 2{,}083{,}333.3 \times 0.02832$$
$$V = 59{,}000 \text{ m}^3$$

3.10 $A \text{ (each brick)} = 20 \times 9 \times 5$
$$= 900 \text{ cm}^3$$
$$= \frac{900}{1{,}000{,}000} \text{ m}^3$$
$$= 0.0009 \text{ m}^3$$
$$A \text{ (brick wall)} = 4.5 \times 1.2 \times 0.5$$
$$= 2.7 \text{ m}^3$$

Number of bricks needed $= \dfrac{2.7}{0.0009}$
$= 3{,}000$ bricks

3.11 $A = 6a^2$
$$660 = 6a^2$$
$$\frac{660}{6} = a^2$$
$$a^2 = 110$$
$$\sqrt{a^2} = \sqrt{110}$$
$$a = 10.49 \text{ in.}$$
$$a = 10.49 \times 2.54$$
$$a = 26.64 \text{ cm}$$

3.12 $V = \tfrac{4}{3}\pi r^3 = \tfrac{1}{6}\pi d^3$
$$V = \tfrac{1}{6}(3.14)(2\tfrac{11}{16})^3$$
$$V = \tfrac{1}{6}(3.14)(2.6875)^3$$
$$V = \tfrac{1}{6}(3.14)(19.4109)$$
$$V = 10.16 \text{ in.}^3$$

3.13 5 liters $= 5{,}000 \text{ cm}^3$
$$= \frac{5{,}000}{1{,}000{,}000} \text{ m}^3$$
$$= .005 \text{ m}^3$$
$$= .005 \times \frac{1}{2.832 \times 10^{-2}} \text{ ft.}^3$$
$$= .005 \times \frac{1}{.02832} \text{ ft.}^3$$
$$= 0.17655 \text{ ft.}^3$$
$$= 0.17655 \times 1728 \text{ in.}^3$$
$$= 305.0784 \text{ in.}^3$$

3.13 cont.

V (square slab) $= abc$
$= 1''(bc)$
$= 1''(\text{side})^2$
$= 1''(a)^2$
$= a^2$

$a^2 = 305.0784$
$\sqrt{a^2} = \sqrt{305.0784}$
$a = 17.47$ in.; slab would be 17.47" x 17.47"

3.14 $V = \frac{4}{3}\pi r^3 = \frac{1}{6}\pi d^3$
$V = \frac{1}{6}(3.14)(3.5)^3$
$V = \frac{1}{6}(3.14)(42.875)$
$V = \frac{1}{6}(134.6275)$
$V = 22.4379$ ft.^{3}

$V = 22.4379 \times 1{,}728$ in.^{3}
$V = 38{,}772.69$ in.^{3}
$V = 38{,}772.69 \times 0.26$
$V = 10{,}080.89$ or 10,081 lbs.

3.15 $A = 4\pi r^2$
$r = \frac{1}{2}(10.5) = 5.25$ ft.
$A = 4(3.14)(5.25)^2$
$A = 4(3.14)(27.5625)$
$A = 346.2$ ft.^{2}

3.16 $V = 35 \times 20 \times 5 = 3{,}500$ ft.^{3}
$3{,}500 \times 7\frac{1}{2} = 26{,}250$ gallons

3.17 $26{,}250 \div 400 = 65.625 = 66$ min.

3.18 V (rod) $= \pi r^2 h$
$r = \frac{1}{2}(\frac{3}{4}) = \frac{3}{8}''$
$h = 12(12) = 144''$
$V = 3.14(\frac{3}{8})^2(144)$
$V = 3.14(0.140625)(144)$
$V = 63.585$ in.^{3}
$V = \frac{63.585}{1{,}728}$ ft.^{3}
$V = 0.036797$ ft.^{3}

$0.036797(490) = 18.03$ lb.

3.19 9 in. $= \frac{3}{4}$ ft. or 0.75 ft.
12 in. = 1 ft.
$V = 150 \times 0.75 \times 1 = 112.5$ ft.^{3}

3.20 $112.5 \times \$0.75 = \$84.38$

3.21 3 in. $= \frac{1}{4}$ ft. or 0.25 ft.
$V = 36 \times 18 \times 0.25$
$V = 162$ ft.^{3}
$V = \frac{162}{27}$ yd.^{3}
$V = 6$ yd.^{3}

3.22 650(6) = 3,900 lb. cement
1,300(6) = 7,800 lb. sand
1,700(6) = 10,200 lb. gravel

3.23 V (wall) $= 60 \times \frac{3}{4} \times 6 = 270$ ft.^{3}
Number of cement blocks needed = 270 x 10 = 2,700 blocks

3.24 $\frac{75(2{,}700)}{1{,}000} = \$202.50$

3.25 $C = \pi d$
$= 3.14(0.5)$
$= 1.57$ in.
Number of coils per inch = 32
Coils to cover rod = 32 x 6
= 192
Length of wire needed = 1.57(192)
= 301.44 in.
$= \frac{301.44}{12}$ ft.
= 25.12 ft. or 25' 2"

3.26 35' x 20' x 6'

3.27 $V = 35 \times 20 \times 6 = 4{,}200$ ft.^{3}

3.28 A (length of cool deck)
$= 2 \times 45 \times 5 = 450$ ft.^{2}
A (width of cool deck)
$= 2 \times 30 \times 5 = 300$ ft.^{2}
A (corners) $= 4 \times 5 \times 5$
$= 100$ ft.^{2}

Add areas of length and width:
$450 + 300 = 750$ ft.^{2}
Subtract areas of corners:
$750 - 100 = 650$ ft.^{2}

or

3.28 cont.

A (length of cool deck)
$= 2 \times 35 \times 5 = 350$ ft.^{2}
A (width of cool deck)
$= 2 \times 20 \times 5 = 200$ ft.^{2}
A (corners) $= 4 \times 5 \times 5 = 100$ ft.^{2}

Add all three measurements:
$350 + 200 + 100 = 650$ ft.^{2}

3.29 3 in. $= \frac{1}{4}$ ft. or 0.25 ft.
$650 \times 0.25 = 162.5$ ft.^{3}

3.30 24(162.5) = 3,900 lb. cement
48(162.5) = 7,800 lb. sand
63(162.5) = 10,237.5 lb. gravel

I. SECTION ONE

1.1
$$\begin{array}{r} \$15.00 \\ -\ 12.82 \\ \hline \$\ 2.18 \end{array}$$

1.2
$$\begin{array}{r} \$10.00 \\ -\ \ 6.98 \\ \hline \$\ 3.02 \end{array}$$

1.3
$$\begin{array}{r} \$5.00 \\ -\ 3.84 \\ \hline \$1.16 \end{array}$$

1.4
$$\begin{array}{r} \$5.00 \\ -\ 4.00 \\ \hline \$1.00 \end{array}$$

1.5
$$\begin{array}{r} \$20.00 \\ -\ 18.50 \\ \hline \$\ 1.50 \end{array}$$

1.6
$$\begin{array}{r} \$10.07 \\ -\ \ 9.37 \\ \hline \$\ 0.70 \end{array}$$

1.7
$$\begin{array}{r} \$\ 13.00 \\ \times\ 0.05 \\ \hline \$0.6500 \end{array} = \$0.65$$

1.8
$$\begin{array}{r} \$\ \ 7.50 \\ \times\ 0.06 \\ \hline \$0.4500 \end{array} = \$0.45$$

1.9
$$\begin{array}{r} \$\ \ 7.95 \\ \times\ 0.04 \\ \hline \$0.3180 \end{array} = \$0.32$$

1.10
$$\begin{array}{r} \$\ \ 2.95 \\ \times\ 0.05 \\ \hline \$0.1475 \end{array} = \$0.15$$

$$\begin{array}{r} \$\ 8.00 \\ 2.95 \\ +\ \ 0.15 \\ \hline \$11.10 \end{array}$$

1.11
$$\begin{array}{r} \$\ \ 5.75 \\ \times\ 0.04 \\ \hline \$0.2300 \end{array} = \$0.23$$

$$\begin{array}{r} \$13.00 \\ 5.75 \\ +\ \ 0.23 \\ \hline \$18.98 \end{array}$$

1.12 $\$8.50 \times 1\frac{1}{2} = 8.50 \times 1.5 =$ $\$12.75$ for labor

$\$1.05 \times 5 = \$5.25$ for oil

$\$5.25 \times 0.06 = \$0.315 = \$0.32$ tax

$\$12.75 + \$5.25 + \$0.32 = \$18.32$

1.13
$$\begin{aligned} I &= \frac{2(12 \times 158.15)}{2{,}500(36 + 1)} \\ &= \frac{2(1{,}897.8)}{2{,}500(37)} \\ &= \frac{3{,}795.6}{92{,}500} \\ &= 0.041 \\ &= 4.1\% \end{aligned}$$

1.14
$$\begin{aligned} I &= \frac{2(12 \times 88.18)}{1{,}100(18 + 1)} \\ &= \frac{2(1{,}058.16)}{1{,}100(19)} \\ &= \frac{2{,}116.32}{20{,}900} \\ &= 0.101 \\ &= 10.1\% \end{aligned}$$

1.15
$$0.18 = \frac{2(12 \times c)}{600(24 + 1)}$$
$$0.18 = \frac{2(12c)}{600(25)}$$
$$0.18 = \frac{24c}{15{,}000}$$
$$\frac{0.18(15{,}000)}{24} = c$$
$$\frac{2{,}700}{24} = c$$
$$c = \$112.50$$

1.16 $0.12 = \frac{2(12 \times c)}{275(18 + 1)}$

$0.12 = \frac{2(12c)}{275(19)}$

$0.12 = \frac{24c}{5,225}$

$\frac{0.12(5,225)}{24} = c$

$\frac{627}{24} = c$

$c = 26.125 = \$26.13$

1.17 $I = 18\% = 0.18$
$y = 12$
$m = \$5,955.00 - 500$
$= \$5,455.00$
$n = 48$

Find c:

$0.18 = \frac{2(12 \times c)}{5,455(48 + 1)}$

$0.18 = \frac{2(12c)}{5,455(49)}$

$0.18 = \frac{24c}{267,295}$

$\frac{0.18(267,295)}{24} = c$

$\frac{48,113.1}{24} = c$

$c = \$2,004.71$

$\text{Monthly payments} = \frac{5,455 + 2,004.71}{48}$

$= \frac{7,459.71}{48}$

$= \$155.41$

1.18 Total payments made for 36 months = 36 x \$104.50 = \$3,762.

Total amount of interest = \$3,762 - 3,500 = \$262.

$y = 12$
$c = \$262$
$m = \$3,500$
$n = 36$

1.18 cont.

$I = \frac{2(12 \times 262)}{3,500(36 + 1)}$

$= \frac{2(3,144)}{3,500(37)}$

$= \frac{6,288}{129,500}$

$= 0.049$

$= 4.9\%$

1.19 \$15.75 x 0.125 = 1.96875 = \$1.97

1.20 \$4,595 x 0.15 = \$689.25

1.21 \$45 ÷ \$475 = 0.095 = 9.5%

1.22 \$35 ÷ 0.1 = \$350

1.23 \$415.80(1 - 0.2) =
\$415.80(0.8) = \$332.64

1.24 (% discount)(\$19.95)
= \$19.95 - 17.85
(% discount)(\$19.95)
= \$2.10

$\% \text{ discount} = \frac{\$2.10}{\$19.95}$

$= 0.105$

$= 10.5\%$

1.25 price = (\$38.75 x .10) + \$38.75
= \$ 3.875 + \$38.75
= \$42.62

1.26 price = (\$138.25 x .125) + \$138.25
= \$17.28 + \$138.25
= \$155.53

1.27 \$63.00 = (\$58.00 x markup) + \$58.00
\$63.00 - \$58.00 = \$58.00 x markup

$\frac{\$5.00}{\$58.00} = \text{markup}$

markup = .086 = 9%

1.28

Let x = cost

$75.50 = .05x + x

$75.50 = 1.05x

$\frac{\$75.50}{1.05} = x = \$71.90$

1.29

$1,595 = ($1,435 x markup) + $1,435

$1,595 - $1,435 = $1,435 x markup

$\frac{\$160}{\$1,435}$ = markup

markup = .111 = 11%

1.30 First 8 hours:
Service charge = $6.50 x 8
= $52.00

Price = ($52.00 x .15) + $52.00
= $7.80 + $52.00
= $59.80

Second 8 hours:
Service charge = $6.50 x 8
= $52.00

Price = ($52.00 x .10) + $52.00
= $5.20 + $52.00
= $57.20

Total price = $59.80 + $57.20
= $117.00

II. SECTION TWO

2.1 10,000 x 2.1¢ = $210

2.2 First year:
15,000 x 4.6¢ = $690
Second year:
15,000 x 4.0¢ = $600
Third year:
15,000 x 3.4¢ = $510

Total depreciation
= $690 + 600 + 510
= $1,800

2.3 First year:
16,500 x 0.7¢ = $115.50
Second year:
15,500 x 1.0¢ = $155

Total cost = $115.50 + 155
= $270.50 or $271

2.4 14,000 x 1.1¢ = $154

2.5 First year:
15,000 x 11.2¢ = $1,680
Second year:
14,000 x 10.2¢ = $1,428
Third year:
13,000 x 10.6¢ = $1,378

Total costs = $1,680 + 1,428 +
1,378
= $4,486

2.6 $2,995 x 10% =
$2,995 x 0.1 = $299.50

2.7 $3,850 x 25% =
$3,850 x 0.25 = $962.50

2.8 $9,550 x 50% =
$9,550 x 0.5 = $4,775

2.9 $3,500 x 10% =
$3,500 x 0.1 = $350

2.10 Market
value = $5,500 x 5%
= $5,500 x 0.05
= $275

2.10 cont.

Maintenance and repair costs $= \$5,500 \times 7.5\%$
$= \$5,500 \times 0.075$
$= \$412.50$

Difference $= \$275 - \$412.50$
$= -\$137.50$

2.11 1967

2.12 Accidents in 1965: 250
Accidents in 1966: 310
Accidents in 1967: 300
Accidents in 1968: 375
Accidents in 1969: 400
Accidents in 1970: 425
Total accidents: 2,060

2.13 Accidents in 1966: 310
Accidents in 1967: 300

Percentage decrease $= \frac{310 - 300}{300}$
$= \frac{10}{300}$
$= 0.03$
$= 3\%$

2.14 Percentage increase for 1965 to 1966 $= \frac{310 - 250}{250}$
$= \frac{60}{250}$
$= 0.24$
$= 24\%$

Percentage increase for 1967 to 1968 $= \frac{375 - 300}{300}$
$= \frac{75}{300}$
$= 0.25$
$= 25\%$

Percentage increase for 1968 to 1969 $= \frac{400 - 375}{375}$
$= \frac{25}{375}$
$= 0.07$
$= 7\%$

2.14 cont.

Percentage increase for 1969 to 1970 $= \frac{425 - 400}{400}$
$= \frac{25}{400}$
$= 0.06$
$= 6\%$

The years that had the greatest percentage increase were 1967 and 1968.

2.15 25%

2.16 Accidents in 1970: 425
Accidents in 1965: 250
Difference $= 425 - 250 = 175$

2.17 Area of restaurant $= 100 \times 35$
$= 3,500 \text{ ft.}^2$

Number of seats $= \frac{3,500}{20}$
$= 175$

2.18 $110 \times 20 = 2,200 \text{ ft.}^2$

2.19 Dining area $= 75 \times 20$
$= 1,500 \text{ ft.}^2$

Kitchen and storage area $= \frac{1}{3} \times 1,500$
$= 500 \text{ ft.}^2$

Total space $= 1,500 + 500$
$= 2,000 \text{ ft.}^2$

2.20 Additional dining area $= 60 \times 20$
$= 1,200 \text{ ft.}^2$

Additional kitchen and storage area $= \frac{1}{3} \times 1,200$
$= 400 \text{ ft.}^2$

2.21 Area of garage $= 160 \times 110$
$= 17,600 \text{ ft.}^2$

Space available for parking $= \frac{17,600}{2}$
$= 8,800 \text{ ft.}^2$

2.21 cont.

Number of automobiles $= \frac{8,800}{250}$
$= 35.2$
$= 35$

2.22 $110 \times 250 = 27,500$ ft.^{2}

Space needed $= 2 \times 27,500$
$= 55,000$ ft.^{2}

2.23 Area of garage $= 200 \times 85$
$= 17,000$ ft.^{2}

$86 \times 250 = 21,500$ ft.^{2}
Space needed $= \frac{1}{2} \times 2 \times 21,500$
$= 21,500$ ft.^{2}

Since the space needed is greater than the present area, you do not have sufficient space.

2.24 $\frac{1}{3} \times 48 = 16$
$16 \times 250 = 4,000$ ft.^{2}

Garage area needed $= 2 \times 4,000$
$= 8,000$ ft.^{2}

III. SECTION THREE

3.1 $R = \frac{E}{I} = \frac{18}{36} = 0.5$ ohm

3.2 $R = \frac{E}{I} = \frac{12}{48} = 0.25$ ohm

3.3 $E = RI = 0.1(60) = 6$ volts

3.4 $R = \frac{E}{I} = \frac{120}{50} = 2.4$ ohms

3.5 $1,850 \div 1\frac{2}{3} =$
$1,850 \times \frac{3}{5} = 1,110$ r.p.m.

3.6 $2,100 \div 3 = 700$ r.p.m.

3.7 Since the engine is running at the same speed as the propeller shaft, the transmission is in third gear.

3.8 engine speed $\div 3 = 650$
engine speed $= 3(650)$
$= 1,950$ r.p.m.

3.9 $\frac{d_a}{d_b} = \frac{\text{r.p.m.}_b}{\text{r.p.m.}_a}$

$\frac{3}{4} = \frac{\text{r.p.m.}_b}{2,000}$

$\text{r.p.m.}_b = \frac{3(2,000)}{4}$

$= \frac{6,000}{4}$

$= 1,500$ r.p.m.

3.10 Since pulley C is keyed to pulley B, pulley C is rotating at 1,500 r.p.m.

$\frac{d_c}{d_d} = \frac{\text{r.p.m.}_d}{\text{r.p.m.}_c}$

$\frac{2}{6} = \frac{\text{r.p.m.}_d}{1,500}$

$\text{r.p.m.}_d = \frac{2(1,500)}{6}$

$= \frac{3,000}{6}$

$= 500$ r.p.m.

3.11

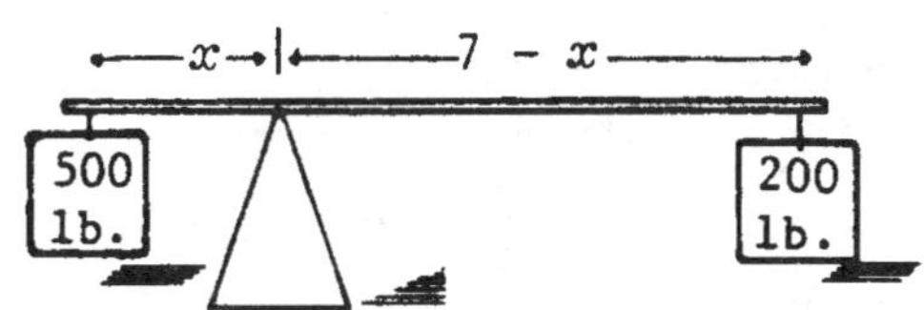

weight$_a$ x distance$_a$ =
weight$_b$ x distance$_b$

$500 \times x = 200 \times (7 - x)$
$500x = 1,400 - 200x$
$500x + 200x = 1,400$
$700x = 1,400$
$\frac{700x}{700} = \frac{1,400}{700}$
$x = 2$ ft.
$7 - x = 7 - 2 = 5$ ft., distance from the 200 lb. weight

3.12 $F \times d_h = W \times d_a$

$F \times 20 = 400 \times 3$

$20F = 1{,}200$

$\frac{20F}{20} = \frac{1{,}200}{20}$

$F = 60$ lb.

3.13 Number of oz. needed = 250 x 4
= 1,000 oz.

Number of cans needed = $\frac{1{,}000}{48}$
= 20.8 or 21 cans

Number of cases needed = $\frac{21}{12}$
= $1\frac{3}{4}$ cases

3.14 Number of cans available = 2 x 12
= 24 cans

Number of oz. in cans = 24 x 44
= 1,056 oz.

Number of patrons = $\frac{1{,}056}{6}$
= 176 patrons

3.15 Number of oz. needed = 225 x 8
= 1,800 oz.

Number of cans needed = $\frac{1{,}800}{45}$
= 40 cans

3.16 $\frac{160}{2.5}$ = 64 lb.

3.17 $\frac{240}{3.5}$ = 68.57 or 69 lb.

3.18 86 x 3.5 = 301 customers

3.19 Converted weight = 165 x 0.45
= 74.25 kg

Amount of protein = 74.25 x 1
= 74.25g

3.20 Converted weight = 112 x 0.45
= 50.4 kg

Amount of protein = 50.4 x 1
= 50.4 g

3.21 69.75 g protein = 69.75 kg weight

Weight in pounds = $\frac{69.75}{0.45}$
= 155 lb.

3.22 174 x $\frac{2}{3}$ = 116 cal.

3.23 135 x 0.62 = 83.7 or 84 cal.

3.24 Calories used = weight x calorie-use factor

90 = 139 x calorie-use factor

$\frac{90}{139}$ = calorie-use factor

calorie-use factor = 0.65
= 65%

Since the 65% calorie-use factor is associated with the 8-minute mile, he must run the mile in 8 minutes.

3.25 Labor cost = \$8.50 x $4\frac{3}{4}$
= \$40.38

Overhead cost = \$40.38 x 0.85
= \$34.32

Cost of parts = \$17.75

Total job cost = \$40.38 + \$34.32 + \$17.75
= \$92.45

3.26 Labor cost = \$7.00 x 15
= \$105.00

Overhead cost = \$105.00 x 1.10
= \$115.50

Cost of parts = \$38.75

Total job cost = \$105.00 + \$115.50 + \$38.75
= \$259.25

3.27 Labor cost = \$8.00 x 6
= \$48.00
Total job cost = \$86.00

$$\text{Overhead rate} = \frac{\$86.00 - 48.00}{\$48.00} = \frac{\$38.00}{\$48.00} = 0.79 = 79\%$$

3.28 Cost of worker A's labor = \$15.00 x $2\frac{1}{2}$
= \$37.50
Cost of worker B's labor = \$8.00 x 1
= \$8.00
Cost of worker C's labor = \$5.25 x $\frac{3}{4}$
= \$3.94

Total labor charges = \$37.50 + 8.00 + 3.94
= \$49.44
Cost of overhead = \$49.44 x 0.75
= \$37.08
Retail price of goods = \$125.50
Total cost of job = \$49.44 + 37.08 + 125.50
= \$212.02

3.29 \$241.98 - 134.75 = \$107.23
Let x = labor cost.

$$\begin{aligned}
\text{labor cost} + \text{overhead cost} &= \$107.23 \\
x + 0.95x &= \$107.23 \\
1x + 0.95x &= \$107.23 \\
1.95x &= \$107.23 \\
\frac{1.95x}{1.95} &= \frac{\$107.23}{1.95} \\
x &= \frac{\$107.23}{1.95} \\
x &= \$54.99
\end{aligned}$$

Hourly labor rate = \$54.99 ÷ $4\frac{1}{2}$
= \$54.99 x $\frac{2}{9}$
= \$12.22 per hour

CONSUMER MATHEMATICS 7
SOLUTION KEY

I. SECTION ONE

1.1

$$c = \$178.25 \times 24 - (\$4{,}250 - \$700)$$
$$= \$4{,}278 - \$3{,}550$$
$$= \$728$$
$$I = \frac{2(12)(728)}{3{,}550(24 + 1)}$$
$$= \frac{2(12)728)}{3{,}550(25)}$$
$$= \frac{17{,}472}{88{,}750}$$
$$= 0.197$$
$$= 19.7\%$$

1.2

$$c = \$198.75 \times 36 - (\$6{,}650 - \$2{,}000)$$
$$= \$7{,}155 - \$4{,}650$$
$$= \$2{,}505$$
$$I = \frac{2(12)(2{,}505)}{4{,}650(36 + 1)}$$
$$= \frac{2(12)(2{,}505)}{4{,}650(37)}$$
$$= \frac{60{,}120}{172{,}050}$$
$$= 0.349$$
$$= 34.9\%$$

1.3

$$0.12 = \frac{2(12)c}{(3{,}875 - 385)(30 + 1)}$$
$$0.12 = \frac{2(12)c}{3{,}490(31)}$$
$$\frac{0.12(3{,}490)(31)}{2(12)} = c$$
$$\frac{12{,}982.8}{24} = c$$
$$c = \$540.95$$

Amount of monthly payments =

$$\frac{3{,}490 + 540.95}{30} =$$
$$\frac{4{,}030.95}{30} = \$134.37$$

1.4

$$0.2 = \frac{2(12)c}{(5{,}200 - 550)(42 + 1)}$$
$$0.2 = \frac{2(12)c}{4{,}650(43)}$$
$$\frac{0.2(4{,}650)(43)}{2(12)} = c$$
$$\frac{39{,}990}{24} = c$$
$$c = \$1{,}666.25$$

Amount of monthly payments =

$$\frac{4{,}650 + 1{,}666.25}{42} =$$
$$\frac{6{,}316.25}{42} = \$150.39$$

1.5

$$0.09 = \frac{2(12)(155 \times 48 - m)}{m(48 + 1)}$$
$$0.09 = \frac{2(12)(7{,}440 - m)}{m(49)}$$
$$0.09 = \frac{24(7{,}440 - m)}{49m}$$
$$0.09(49m) = 24(7{,}440 - m)$$
$$4.41m = 178{,}560 - 24m$$
$$4.41m + 24m = 178{,}560$$
$$28.41m = 178{,}560$$
$$\frac{28.41m}{28.41} = \frac{178{,}560}{28.41}$$
$$m = \$6{,}285.11$$

Down payment = \$6,995 - \$6,285.11
= \$709.89 or \$710

1.6

$$0.185 = \frac{2(12)(681.51)}{m(30 + 1)}$$
$$0.185 = \frac{2(12)(681.51)}{m(31)}$$
$$0.185(m)(31) = 2(12)(681.51)$$
$$m = \frac{2(12)(681.51)}{0.185(31)}$$
$$= \frac{16{,}356.24}{5.735}$$
$$= \$2{,}852$$

1.7 $\frac{\$1{,}200}{12{,}500} = 0.096 = 9.6¢$

1.8 $\frac{\$1.024}{8¢} = \frac{\$1{,}024}{\$0.08} = 12{,}800$ miles

1.9 Gallons purchased = $\frac{14,500}{15.5}$ = 935.48

Cost of gasoline = 935.48 x 0.669 = \$625.84

Cost of oil = \$8.75

Total cost of gasoline and oil = \$625.84 + \$8.75 = \$634.59

Cost per mile for gasoline and oil = $\frac{\$634.59}{14,500}$ = 0.044 = 4.4¢ per mile

1.10 Total cost of operating costs listed = \$225 + \$165 + \$312 = \$702

Operating cost = $\frac{\$702}{17,500}$ = 0.04 = 4¢ per mile

1.11 Cost of maintenance = \$8.50 x 12 = \$102

Total operating cost = \$55 + \$3.50 + \$102 = \$160.50

Operating cost = $\frac{\$160.50}{13,000}$ = 0.012 = 1.2¢ per mile

1.12 Total operating cost = \$0 + \$165 + \$155 = \$320

Miles driven = $\frac{\$320}{\$0.032}$ = 10,000 miles

1.13 Total depreciation = \$5,750 - \$3,250 = \$2,500

Average yearly depreciation = $\frac{\$2,500}{4}$ = \$625 per year

1.13 cont.

Cost of depreciation = $\frac{\$625}{16,025}$ = 0.039 = 3.9¢ per mile

1.14 Total depreciation = \$3,850 - \$150 = \$3,700

Average yearly depreciation = $\frac{\$3,700}{9}$ = \$411.11 per year

Cost of depreciation = $\frac{\$411.11}{18,000}$ = 0.023 = 2.3¢ per mile

1.15 Total depreciation = \$6,600 - \$3,900 = \$2,700

Average yearly depreciation = $\frac{\$2,700}{3}$ = \$900

Average number of miles driven per year = $\frac{\$900}{\$0.09}$ = 10,000 miles

1.16 Average yearly depreciation = 15,000 x \$0.085 = \$1,275

Total depreciation = \$1,275 x 5 = \$6,375

Resale value = \$7,885 - \$6,375 = \$1,510

1.17 \$127

1.18 \$145

1.19 $\frac{\$145 - \$127}{\$127} = \frac{\$18}{\$127}$
= 0.142
= 14.2%

1.20 a. At $127 premium the bodily injury coverage is $50,000 for one person. At $145 premium the bodily injury coverage is $250,000 for one person.

Increase in coverage $= \frac{\$250,000 - \$50,000}{\$50,000}$
$= \frac{\$200,000}{\$50,000}$
= 4
= 400%

b. At $127 premium the property damage coverage is $10,000. At $145 premium the bodily injury coverage is $50,000.

Increase in coverage $= \frac{\$50,000 - \$10,000}{\$10,000}$
$= \frac{\$40,000}{\$10,000}$
= 4
= 400%

1.21 $100

1.22 $68

1.23 $\frac{\$100 - \$68}{\$100} = \frac{\$32}{\$100}$
= 0.32
= 32%

1.24 $\frac{\$150 - \$50}{\$50} = \frac{\$100}{\$50}$
= 2
= 200%

1.25 $15

1.26 $10

1.27 $23

1.28 $23 - $10 = $13

1.29 a. $\frac{\$13}{\$10} = 1.3 = 130\%$

b. $\frac{\$10,000 - \$1,000}{\$1,000} =$
$\frac{\$9,000}{\$1,000} =$
9 = 900%

II. SECTION TWO

2.1 $d = rt = 35(2\frac{1}{2}) =$
$35(\frac{5}{2}) = 87.5$ miles

2.2 $d = rt$
$420 = 45t$
$\frac{420}{45} = \frac{45t}{45}$
$t = 9\frac{1}{3}$ hr. or 9 hr., 20 min.

2.3 $d = rt$
$1,505 = 420t$
$\frac{1,505}{420} = \frac{420t}{420}$
$t = 3.58$ hr. or
3 hr., 35 min.

2.4 $d = rt$
$2,400 = 450t$
$\frac{2,400}{450} = \frac{450t}{450}$
$t = 5\frac{1}{3}$ hr. + 35 min.
= 5 hr., 20 min. + 35 min.
= 5 hr., 55 min.

2.5 $d = rt$
$95 = 105t$
$\frac{95}{105} = \frac{105t}{105}$
$t = 0.905$ hr.
= 54.3 minutes

2.6 $d_{\text{car 1}} = d_{\text{car 2}}$, or
$r_{\text{car 1}}t_{\text{car 1}} = r_{\text{car 2}}t_{\text{car 2}}$

$55(t + \frac{4}{60}) = 70t$
$55(t + \frac{1}{15}) = 70t$
$55t + \frac{11}{3} = 70t$
$\frac{11}{3} = 70t - 55t$
$\frac{11}{3} = 15t$
$\frac{\frac{11}{3}}{15} = \frac{15t}{15}$
$t = \frac{11}{45}$ hr.
$= 0.2\overline{4}$ hr.
= 14.7 minutes

2.7 Plane A:
$d = rt = 415(4) = 1{,}660$ miles
Plane B:
$d = rt = 375(4) = 1{,}500$ miles

Distance apart after 4 hours = 1,660 + 1,500
= 3,160 miles

2.8

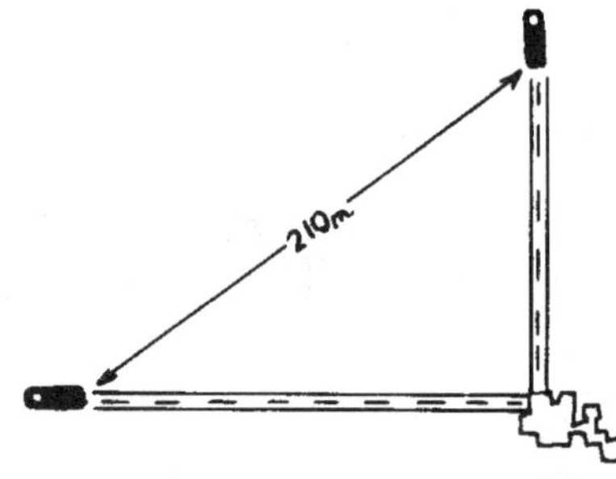

Car 1: $d = rt = 42(3\frac{1}{2})$
$= 147$ miles
Car 2: $d = rt = 50(3)$
$= 150$ miles

$(\text{distance apart})^2 = 147^2 + 150^2 = 21{,}609 + 22{,}500 = 44{,}109$

$\sqrt{(\text{distance apart})^2} = \sqrt{44{,}109}$
distance apart = 210 miles

2.9 The time difference between Chicago and Jerusalem is 8 hours (11:00 a.m. to 7:00 p.m.). Add 8 hours to 6 p.m.; the time in Jerusalem is 2 a.m. the following day.

2.10 The time difference between Honolulu and Moscow is 13 hours (7:00 a.m. to 8:00 p.m.). Add 13 hours to 12 noon; Moscow time is 1 a.m. the following day.

2.11 The time difference between Juneau and Sydney is 18 hours (9:00 a.m. to 3:00 a.m. the following day). Add 18 hours to midnight; Sydney time is 6 p.m. the following day.

2.12 Since the flight lasts 2 hours and no time difference exists between Oslo and Warsaw, the traveler will arrive in Warsaw at 9:30 p.m.

2.13 Since the flight lasts 20 hours and San Francisco is 9 hours earlier than Rome (9:00 a.m. to 6:00 p.m.), the traveler will arrive in San Francisco at 8:00 a.m. + 20 hours - 9 hours, or 8:00 a.m. + 11 hours, or 7:00 p.m. the same day.

2.14 Since New York and Seattle are both on Daylight-Saving Time, and Seattle is 3 hours earlier than New York (9:00 a.m. to 12 noon), Seattle time is 4 p.m. - 3 hours, or 1 p.m.

2.15 The trip took 16 hours + 8 hours, or 24 hours. Add 24 hours to 12 noon, making the time 12 noon the next day. Since Muncie is on Standard Time and New York City is on Daylight-Saving Time, when the time is 12 noon in Muncie, it is 1 p.m. in New York City. Arrival time in New York City is 1 p.m. the following day.

III. SECTION THREE

3.1 5,000(.0439) = \$219.50

3.2 100(18.46) = \$1,846 pounds

3.3 2,000(.6013) = \$1,202.60 United States dollars
\$1,202.60(2.0500) = 2,465.33 guilders

3.4 100,000(.0521) = \$5,210

3.5 1970: 23.20
1976: 40.01

$$\text{Percentage change} = \frac{40.01 - 23.20}{23.20} = \frac{16.81}{23.20} = 0.725 = 72.5\%$$

3.6 appreciated

3.7 1956: 101.60
1976: 101.41

$$\text{Percentage change} = \frac{101.60 - 101.41}{101.60} = \frac{0.19}{101.60} = 0.0019 = 0.19\%$$

3.8 depreciated

3.9 Regular Economy Air Fare = $440.80
Charter Group Air Fare = 331.00
$109.80

3.10 Peak Season Economy Air Fare = $526.30
Regular Economy Air Fare = 440.80
$ 85.50

$$\frac{\$85.50}{\$440.80} = 0.194 = 19.4\%$$

3.11 First-Class Ship Fare = $775.20
Tourist Class Ship Fare = 408.00
$367.20

$$\frac{\$367.20}{\$408.00} = 0.9 = 90\%$$

3.12 1974; 1,301

3.13 1974: 1,301
1975: 441
860

$$\frac{860}{1,301} = 0.66 = 66\%$$

3.14 1976: 82
1966: 51
31

$$\frac{31}{51} = 0.608 = 60.8\%$$

3.15 1976: 372
1966: 301
71

$$\frac{71}{301} = 0.236 = 23.6\%$$

3.16 1976: 831
1966: 711
120

$$\frac{120}{711} = 0.169 = 16.9\%$$

16.9% is less than 33.3%; therefore, the statement is not true.

3.17 $$\frac{\$20.70 + \$25.00}{2} = \frac{\$45.70}{2} = \$22.85$$

3.18 higher ($22.85 is higher than $22.00)

3.19 Brazil: $18.33 - $12.25 = $6.08
Greece: $16.55 - $9.48 = $7.07

Greece has the larger range.

3.20 High:

$$\frac{\$34.48 - \$23.51}{\$34.48} = \frac{\$10.97}{\$34.48} = 0.318 = 31.8\%$$

Medium:

$$\frac{\$22.46 - \$15.73}{\$22.46} = \frac{\$6.73}{\$22.46} = 0.299 = 29.9\%$$

3.21 High:
West Germany = $22.53
Yugoslavia = $10.96

$$\frac{\$22.53}{\$10.96} = 2.1$$

Medium:

West Germany = $14.33
Yugoslavia = $7.38

$$\frac{\$14.33}{\$7.38} = 1.9$$

3.21 cont.

Yes, the typical tourist pays about twice as much per day to reside in West Germany as he would pay in Yugoslavia.

3.22 Since the value of each shirt is $8.50 (which is less than $10), the shirts are duty-free. The dresses cost 3 x $27.50 = $82.50; the cuff links cost $17.50. The total cost of dresses and cuff links is $82.50 + $17.50, or $100. Since the traveler is entitled to $100 worth of articles duty-free, he pays no duty.

3.23 $4,250 - $100 = $4,150
$4,150(6½%) =
$4,150(0.065) = $269.75

3.24 $4,250 + $269.75 = $4,519.75

3.25 Lace shawls: 4 x $25 = $100
Gold jewelry: $150
Chinaware: $215

Apply the $100 exemption to the chinaware. The amount of $115 remains to be figured at the prevailing duty rate.

Duty on shawls = $100(42½%)
= $100(0.425)
= $42.50
Duty on jewelry = $150(24%)
= $150(0.24)
= $36.00
Duty on chinaware = $115(35%)
= $115(0.35)
= $40.25
Total amount of duty = $42.50 + $36.00 + $40.25
= $118.75

3.26 Total cost of articles = $100 + $150 + $215
= $465

$\frac{\$118.75}{\$465} = 0.255 = 25.5\%$

3.27 Cost by buying goods in Latin America:
Shawls: $100 + $42.50 = $142.50
Jewelry: $150 + $36 = $186.00
Chinaware: $215 + $40.25 = $255.25
Total cost = $142.50 + $186.00 + $255.25
= $583.75

Cost by buying goods in the United States:

Shawls: price $= \frac{\$100}{1.00 - 0.3} = \frac{\$100}{0.7} = \$142.86$

Jewelry: price $= \frac{\$150}{1.00 - 0.3} = \frac{\$150}{0.7} = \$214.29$

Chinaware: price $= \frac{\$215}{1.00 - 0.3} = \frac{\$215}{0.7} = \$307.14$

Total cost = $142.86 + $214.29 + $307.14
= $664.29

No; you would save more by buying the goods in Latin America.

CONSUMER MATHEMATICS 8
SOLUTION KEY

1. SECTION ONE

1.1

Assets	
Cash	$3,605($3,570 + $35)
Accounts Receivable	55($0 + $55)
Equipment	5,750
Total Assets	$9,410

Liabilities	
Accounts Payable	$3,500
Owner's Equity	
Investment	5,910($5,820 + $90)
Total Liabilities and Owner's Equity	$9,410

1.2

Assets	
Cash	$3,355($3,605 - $250)
Accounts Receivable	55
Equipment	5,750
Total Assets	$9,160

Liabilities	
Accounts Payable	$3,250($3,500 - $250)
Owner's Equity	
Investment	5,910
Total Liabilities and Owner's Equity	$9,160

1.3

Assets	
Cash	$2,905($3,355 - $450)
Accounts Receivable	55
Equipment	6,200($5,750 + $450)
Total Assets	$9,160

Liabilities	
Accounts Payable	$3,250
Owner's Equity	
Investment	5,910
Total Liabilities and Owner's Equity	$9,160

1.4

Assets	
Cash	$2,830($2,905 - $75)
Accounts Receivable	55
Equipment	6,200
Total Assets	$9,085

Liabilities	
Accounts Payable	$3,250
Owner's Equity	
Investment	5,835($5,910 - $75)
Total Liabilities and Owner's Equity	$9,085

1.5

Assets	
Cash	$2,830
Accounts Receivable	55
Equipment	7,015($6,200 + $815)
Total Assets	$9,900

Liabilities	
Accounts Payable	$4,065($3,250 + $815)
Owner's Equity	
Investment	5,835
Total Liabilities and Owner's Equity	$9,900

1.6

Assets	
Cash	$ 2,830
Accounts Receivable	1,555($55 + $1,500)
Equipment	7,015
Total Assets	$11,400

Liabilities	
Accounts Payable	$ 4,065
Owner's Equity	
Investments	7,335($5,835 + $1,500)
Total Liabilities and Owner's Equity	$11,400

1.7

Assets	
Cash	$ 2,745($2,830 - $85)
Accounts Receivable	1,555
Equipment	7,015
Total Assets	$11,315

Liabilities	
Accounts Payable	$ 4,065
Owner's Equity	
Investment	7,250($7,335 - $85)
Total Liabilities and Owner's Equity	$11,315

1.8

Assets	
Cash	$ 2,445($2,745 - $300)
Accounts Receivable	1,555
Equipment	7,015
Total Assets	$11,015

Liabilities	
Accounts Payable	$ 4,065
Owner's Equity	
Investment	6,950($7,250 - $300)
Total Liabilities and Owner's Equity	$11,015

1.9

Assets		Liabilities	
Cash	$ 3,395($2,445 + $950)	Accounts Payable	$ 4,065
Accounts Receivable	1,555	Owner's Equity	
Equipment	6,215($7,015 - $800)	Investment	7,100($6,950 + $150)
Total Assets	$11,165	Total Liabilities and Owner's Equity	$11,165

1.10

Assets		Liabilities	
Cash	$ 2,895($3,395 - $500)	Accounts Payable	$ 4,065
Accounts Receivable	1,555	Owner's Equity	
Equipment	6,215	Investment	6,600($7,100 - $500)
Total Assets	$10,665	Total Liabilities and Owner's Equity	$10,665

1.11

Assets		Liabilities	
Cash	$ 2,835($2,895 - $60)	Accounts Payable	$ 4,065
Accounts Receivable	1,555	Owner's Equity	
Equipment	6,215	Investment	6,540($6,600 - $60)
Total Assets	$10,605	Total Liabilities and Owner's Equity	$10,605

1.12

ABC Repair
Balance Sheet
February 29, 1980

Assets		Liabilities + Owner's Equity Liabilities	
Cash	$ 2,835	Accounts Payable	$ 4,065
Accounts Receivable	1,555	Owner's Equity	
Equipment	6,215	Investment	6,540
Total Assets	$10,605	Total Liabilities and Owner's Equity	$10,605

1.13 The beginning balance was $9,320. The ending balance is $10,605. Therefore, your firm made a profit of $10,605 - $9,320, or $1,285.

1.14 cash receipts

1.15 short

1.16 previous

1.17 false

1.18 false

1.19 true

1.20
a. $135 - $110 = ($25)
b. $110 - $85 = ($25)
c. $100 - $95 = $5
d. $130 - $95 = $35
e. $145 - $100 = $45
f. $165 - $105 = $60
g. ($25)
h. ($25) + ($25) = ($50)
i. ($50) + $5 = ($45)
j. ($45) + $35 = ($10)
k. ($10) + $45 = $35
l. $35 + $60 = $95

1.21 May

II. SECTION TWO

2.1
```
  $  498.03
  +  604.28
  $1,102.31
  -  599.49
  $  502.82
```

2.2
```
  $101.90
  + 525.30
  $627.20

  $653.48
  +   5.00
  $658.48
  - 627.20
  ($ 31.28)
```

2.3 e

2.4 d

2.5 a

2.6 b

2.7 c

2.8 f

2.9 9

2.10 3

2.11 $528.56 + $48.38 = $576.94

2.12 $412.56 + $155.00 + $258.38 = $825.94

2.13 $48.38 + $58.58 + $205.38 + $210.88 + $58.28 + $149.39 + $175.38 + $20.88 + $83.50 = $1,010.65

2.14 $5.00

2.15 $387.23

2.16 d

2.17 f

2.18 b

2.19 g

2.20 e

2.21 c

2.22 Claim one less exemption than the number you are legally entitled to.

2.23 Net pay received after all deductions have been made according to federal, state, and local regulations.

III. SECTION THREE

3.1 T.C. = F.C. + V.C.
= $8,900 + 5,000($5.50)
= $8,900 + $27,500
= $36,400

3.2 Revenue = 4,600($17.75)
= $81,650

3.3 T.C. = F.C. + V.C.
= $8,900 + 3,750($5.95)
= $8,900 + $22,312.50
= $31,212.50

3.4 Revenue = 3,600($16.50)
= $59,400

3.5 Profit = Revenue - Total Costs
= ($81,650 + $59,400) - ($36,400 + $31,212.50)
= $141,050 - $67,612.50
= $73,437.50

3.6 d

3.7 a

3.8 g

3.9 b

3.10 h

3.11 c

3.12 e

3.13 f

3.14 lower

3.15 false

3.16 true

3.17 true

3.18 $98.65(0.03) = $2.96
$98.65 - $2.96 = $95.69

3.19 $\frac{\text{Amount of interest}}{\text{Amount of loan}}$ = interest rate

$\frac{\text{Amount of interest}}{\$5{,}000}$ = 0.05

Amount of interest = $5,000(0.05)
= $250 per month
= 3($250)
= $750 for 90 days (3 months)

total payment = $5,000 + $750
= $5,750

3.20 Either order:
a. treasury bills
b. 90-day certificates of deposit

3.21 b

3.22 a

3.23 c

3.24 Petroleum: $\frac{11.2 - 9.3}{11.2} = \frac{1.9}{11.2} =$ 0.17 = 17%

Drugs: $\frac{10.8 - 9.4}{10.8} = \frac{1.4}{10.8} =$ 0.13 = 13%

Chemicals: $\frac{8.0 - 5.0}{8.0} = \frac{3.0}{8.0} =$ 0.375 = 37.5%

Motor Vehicles: $\frac{6.2 - 2.4}{6.2} = \frac{3.8}{6.2} =$ 0.613 = 61.3%

3.24 cont.

Electrical: $\frac{4.8 - 3.3}{4.8} =$

$\frac{1.5}{4.8} =$

$0.313 = 31.3\%$

Food: $\frac{2.7 - 2.5}{2.7} =$

$\frac{0.2}{2.7} =$

$0.074 = 7.4\%$

a. food industry
b. 7.4%

3.25 a. motor vehicles industry
b. 61.3%

3.26 price = ($6.95 x .33) + $6.95

= $2.29 + $6.95

= $9.24

3.27 $22.95 = ($17.45 x markup) + $17.45

$22.95 - $17.45 = $17.45 x markup

$\frac{\$5.50}{\$17.45} = \text{markup}$

markup = .315 = 32%

3.28 $\frac{\$19.95 - \$15.75}{\$19.95} =$

$\frac{\$4.20}{\$19.95} =$

$0.21 = 21\%$

3.29 let x = cost

$129.95 = .15x + x

$129.95 = 1.15 x

$\frac{\$129.95}{1.15} = \$113$

3.30 Amount of discount = $129.95(0.18)
= $23.39

Price = $129.95 - $23.39
= $106.56

CONSUMER MATHEMATICS 9
SOLUTION KEY

I. SECTION ONE

1.1 $\frac{\frac{14}{7}}{\frac{21}{7}} = \frac{2}{3}$

1.2 The lowest common denominator = 18;
$\frac{2}{3} = \frac{12}{18}$, $\frac{5}{6} = \frac{15}{18}$, and $\frac{10}{18} = \frac{10}{18}$.
$\frac{12}{18} + \frac{15}{18} + \frac{10}{18} = \frac{37}{18}$ or $2\frac{1}{18}$

1.3 $\frac{6}{4} = \frac{3}{2}$ or 3:2

1.4 $4 \times C = 6 \times 8$
$4C = 48$
$\frac{4C}{4} = \frac{48}{4}$
$C = 12$

1.5 b

1.6 a

1.7 e

1.8 d

1.9 c

1.10 $1{:}50 = d{:}75$
$50 \times d = 1 \times 75$
$50d = 75$
$\frac{50d}{50} = \frac{75}{50}$
$d = 1\frac{1}{2}$ inches

1.11 $1{:}10 = 1\frac{1}{4}{:}d$
$10 \times 1\frac{1}{4} = 1 \times d$
$\frac{25}{2} = d$
$d = 12\frac{1}{2}$ km

1.12 a. Length:
$10'\ 6'' = 120'' + 6'' = 126''$
$\frac{1}{4}{:}12 = l{:}126$
$12 \times l = \frac{1}{4} \times 126$
$12l = \frac{63}{2}$
$\frac{12l}{12} = \frac{\frac{63}{2}}{12}$
$l = \frac{63}{24} = 2\frac{5}{8}''$

Width:
$11' = 132''$
$\frac{1}{4}{:}12 = w{:}132$
$12 \times w = \frac{1}{4} \times 132$
$12w = 33$
$\frac{12w}{12} = \frac{33}{12}$
$w = \frac{33}{12} = \frac{11}{4} = 2\frac{3}{4}''$
Scale dimensions are $2\frac{5}{8}''$ by $2\frac{3}{4}''$.

b. Length:
$25' = 300''$
$\frac{1}{4}{:}12 = l{:}300$
$12 \times l = \frac{1}{4} \times 300$
$12l = 75$
$\frac{12l}{12} = \frac{75}{12}$
$l = \frac{75}{12} = \frac{25}{4} = 6\frac{1}{4}''$

Width:
$18'\ 8'' = 216'' + 8'' = 224''$
$\frac{1}{4}{:}12 = w{:}224$
$12 \times w = \frac{1}{4} \times 224$
$12w = 56$
$\frac{12w}{12} = \frac{56}{12}$
$w = \frac{56}{12} = \frac{14}{3} = 4\frac{2}{3}''$
Scale dimensions are $6\frac{1}{4}''$ by $4\frac{2}{3}''$.

c. Length:
$13'\ 6'' = 156'' + 6'' = 162''$
$\frac{1}{4}{:}12 = l{:}162$
$12 \times l = \frac{1}{4} \times 162$
$12l = \frac{81}{2}$
$\frac{12l}{12} = \frac{\frac{81}{2}}{12}$
$l = \frac{81}{24} = \frac{27}{8} = 3\frac{3}{8}''$

1.12 cont.

Width:

$8' = 96''$

$\frac{1}{4}:12 = w:96$

$12 \times w = \frac{1}{4} \times 96$

$12w = 24$

$\frac{12w}{12} = \frac{24}{12}$

$w = 2''$

Scale dimensions are $3\frac{3}{8}''$ by 2".

d. Length:

$12' = 144''$

$\frac{1}{4}:12 = l:144$

$12 \times l = \frac{1}{4} \times 144$

$12l = 36$

$\frac{12l}{12} = \frac{36}{12}$

$l = 3''$

Width:

$10' = 120''$

$\frac{1}{4}:12 = w:120$

$12 \times w = \frac{1}{4} \times 120$

$12w = 30$

$\frac{12w}{12} = \frac{30}{12}$

$w = \frac{30}{12} = \frac{5}{2} = 2\frac{1}{2}''$

Scale dimensions are 3" by $2\frac{1}{2}''$.

1.13 621333

1.14 500 ft.

1.15 contours

1.16 lower left

1.17 gentle

1.18 tenths

1.19 c

1.20 d

1.21 e

1.22 b

1.23 10" + 6" + 8" = 24"

1.24

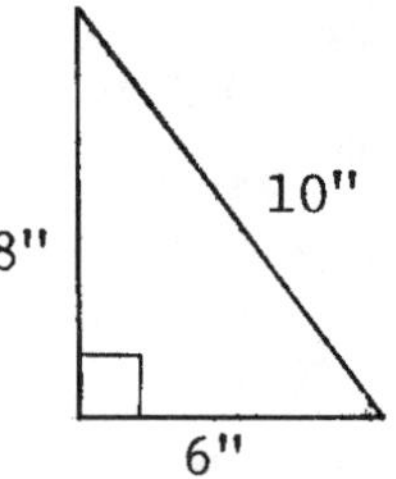

$A = \frac{1}{2}bh$

$= \frac{1}{2}(6)(8)$

$= 24 \text{ in.}^2$

or

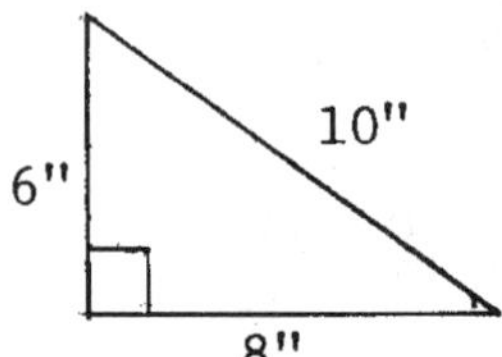

$A = \frac{1}{2}bh$

$= \frac{1}{2}(8)(6)$

$= 24 \text{ in.}^2$

1.25 $A = 100(20) = 2{,}000 \text{ ft.}^2$

1.26 $P = 100 + 20 + 100 + 20$

$= 240 \text{ ft.}$

1.27 $P = 50 + (15 + 20) + 30 + 20 + (50 - 30) + 15$

$= 50 + 35 + 30 + 20 + 20 + 15$

$= 170 \text{ ft.}$

1.28

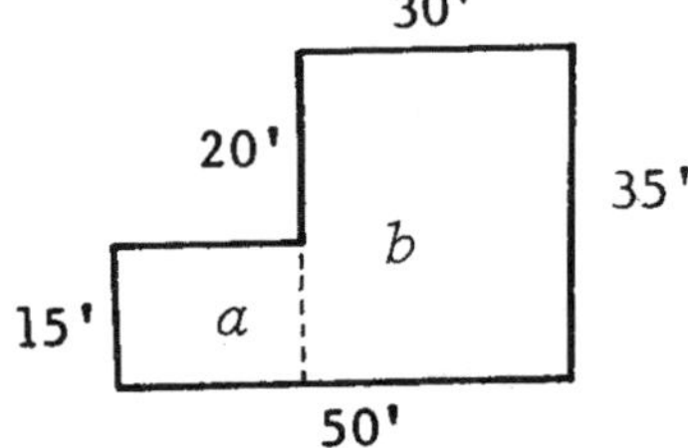

$A_a = 20(15) = 300 \text{ ft.}^2$

$A_b = 35(30) = 1{,}050 \text{ ft.}^2$

Total area $= 300 + 1{,}050$

$= 1{,}350 \text{ ft.}^2$

II. SECTION TWO

2.1

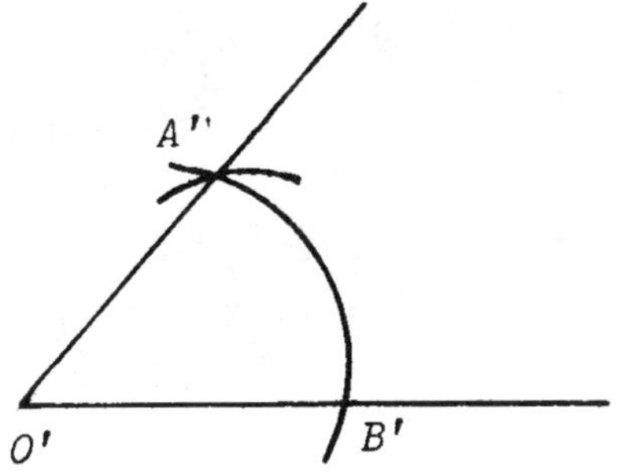

2.2

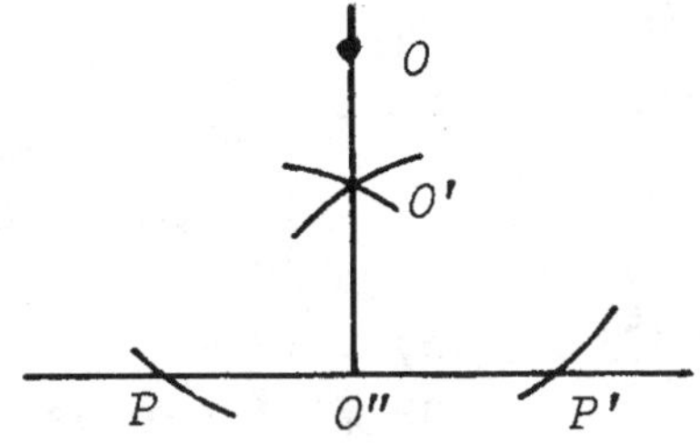

2.3

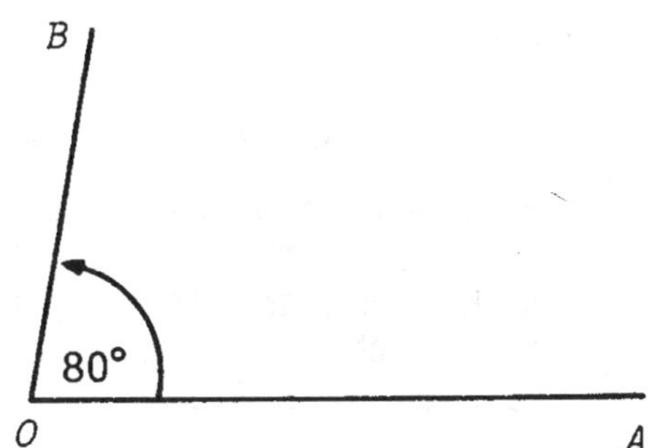

2.4 310° - 180° = 130°;
310° is 130° more than 180°

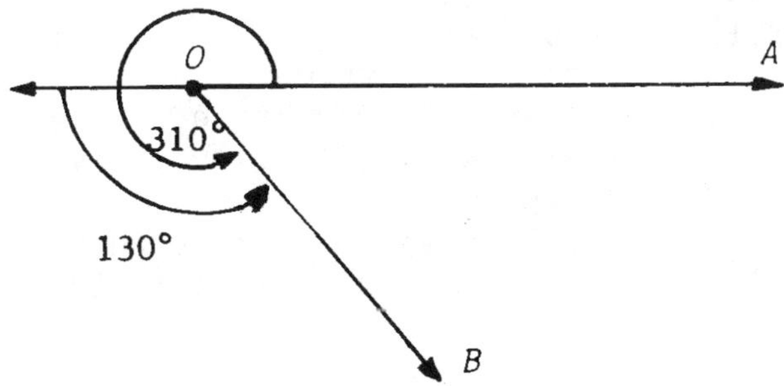

2.5 false

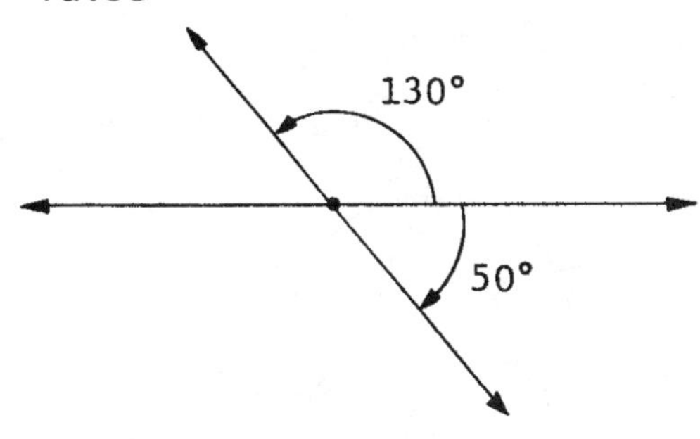

2.6 true

2.7 false

2.8 true

2.9 obtuse angle

2.10 perpendicular

2.11 protractor

2.12 shortest line

2.13 decagon

2.14 Either order:
a. equilateral
b. equiangular

2.15 interior

2.16 equilateral triangle

2.17 $(1 - \frac{2}{5}) \times 180° = \frac{3}{5} \times 180° = 108°$

2.18 $(1 - \frac{2}{12}) \times 180° = \frac{5}{6} \times 180° = 150°$

2.19 $(7 - 2) \times 180° = 5 \times 180° = 900°$

2.20 $(10 - 2) \times 180° = 8 \times 180° = 1{,}440°$

2.21 $A = 2.598(2)^2$
$= 2.598(4)$
$= 10.392 \text{ in.}^2$

2.22 $A = 6.182(5)^2$
$= 6.182(25)$
$= 154.55 \text{ in.}^2$

2.23 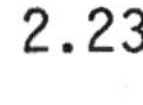

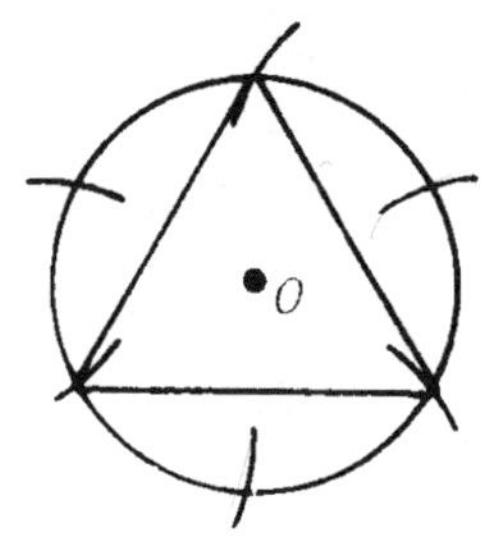

2.24

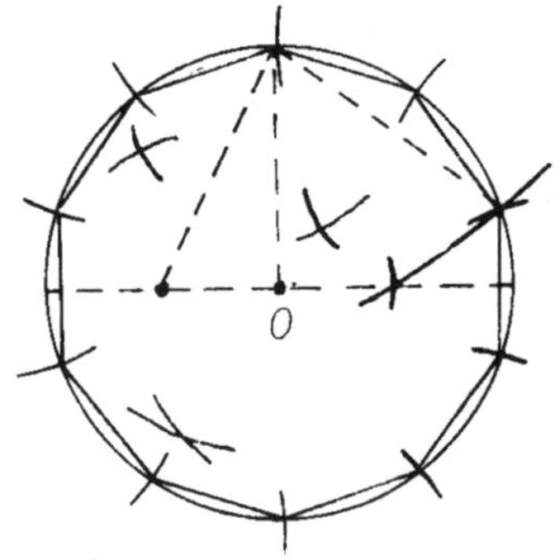

2.25 c

2.26 a

2.27 e

2.28 b

2.29 d

III. SECTION THREE

3.1 false

3.2 true

3.3 false

3.4 true

3.5 true

3.6 Total space for 7-member family = 1,603 - 1,858 ft.^{2}.

$\frac{1,603 + 1,858}{2} = \frac{3,461}{2}$
= 1,730.5 average sq. ft.

$\frac{1,730.5}{7} = 247.2 \text{ ft.}^2$
$= 247 \text{ ft.}^2$ per person (approximately)

3.7 Total space for family with three teen-agers = 1,388 - 1,589 ft.^{2}.

$\frac{1,388 + 1,589}{2} = \frac{2,977}{2}$
= 1,488.5 average sq. ft.

$\frac{1,488.5}{5} = 297.7 \text{ ft.}^2$
$= 298 \text{ ft.}^2$ per person (approximately)

3.8 35 ft.^{2}

3.9 $\frac{50 + 80}{2} = \frac{130}{2}$
$= 65 \text{ ft.}^2$ on the average

The square root of 65 ft.^{2} is a little more than 8 ft. Since the kitchen should not be square, the average dimensions are 7'6" by 8'8".

3.10 Any three:
a. normal activities that take place
b. size of family
c. ages of family members
d. kinds of furniture, appliances, and possessions

3.11 Any order:
a. ease of service
b. traffic circulation
c. diversity of family activities
d. economy
e. full potential for each room with regard to livability

3.12 c

3.13 d

3.14 a

3.15 b

3.16 c

3.17 a

3.18 d

3.19 d

3.20 a

3.21 b

3.22 c

3.23 f

3.24 e

3.25 false

3.26 false

3.27 true

3.28 true

CONSUMER MATHEMATICS 10
SOLUTION KEY

I. SECTION ONE

1.1 The lowest common denominator is 12.

$$\frac{1}{2} + \frac{1}{4} + \frac{1}{6} + \frac{1}{12} =$$
$$\frac{6}{12} + \frac{3}{12} + \frac{2}{12} + \frac{1}{12} =$$
$$\frac{12}{12} = 1$$

1.2 The lowest common denominator is 20.

$$\frac{19}{20} - \frac{4}{5} =$$
$$\frac{19}{20} - \frac{16}{20} = \frac{3}{20}$$

1.3 $\dfrac{\frac{14}{2}}{\frac{24}{2}} = \dfrac{7}{12}$

1.4 The lowest common denominator is 24.

$$2\tfrac{1}{4} + 3\tfrac{3}{8} + \frac{1}{6} =$$
$$\frac{9}{4} + \frac{27}{8} + \frac{1}{6} =$$
$$\frac{54}{24} + \frac{81}{24} + \frac{4}{24} =$$
$$\frac{139}{24} = 5\tfrac{19}{24}$$

1.5 $\frac{5}{6} \times \frac{1}{12} = \frac{5}{72}$

1.6 $2\tfrac{1}{3} \times \frac{5}{6} =$

$$\frac{7}{3} \times \frac{5}{6} =$$
$$\frac{35}{18} = 1\tfrac{17}{18}$$

1.7 $\frac{4}{7} \div \frac{2}{7} =$

$$\frac{\cancel{4}^{2}}{\cancel{7}_{1}} \times \frac{\cancel{7}^{1}}{\cancel{2}_{1}} = 2$$

1.8 $3\tfrac{1}{5} \div 2\tfrac{3}{10} =$

$$\frac{16}{5} \div \frac{23}{10} =$$
$$\frac{16}{\cancel{5}_{1}} \times \frac{\cancel{10}^{2}}{23} =$$
$$\frac{32}{23} = 1\tfrac{9}{23}$$

1.9
$$\begin{array}{r} 1.38 \\ 1.42 \\ +\ 1.69 \\ \hline 4.49 \end{array}$$

1.10
$$\begin{array}{r} 12.52 \\ -\ \ 4.57 \\ \hline (7.95) \end{array}$$ or -7.95

1.11
$$\begin{array}{r} 1.03 \\ \times\ \ 1.3 \\ \hline 309 \\ 103 \\ \hline 1.339 \end{array}$$

1.12
$$\begin{array}{r} 0.642 \\ 4\overline{)2.568} \\ 24 \\ \hline 16 \\ 16 \\ \hline 08 \\ 8 \\ \hline 0 \end{array}$$

1.13 0.25 x 80 = 20

1.14 0.15 x 14.8 = 2.22

1.15 38 x 0.16 = 6.08
38 - 6.08 = 31.92

1.16 50 x 2.00 = 100
50 + 100 = 150

1.17 $\frac{1}{8}$ = 1 ÷ 8 = 0.125 = 12.5% or $12\tfrac{1}{2}$%

1.18 37.5% or $37\tfrac{1}{2}$%

1.19 $\frac{5}{2} = 2\tfrac{1}{2}$ = 2.5 = 250%

1.20 44.4%

1.21 $4:2 = \frac{4}{2} = \frac{2}{1} = 2:1$

1.22 $3 \text{ to } 9 = 3:9 = \frac{3}{9} = \frac{1}{3} = 1 \text{ to } 3$

1.23 $\frac{17}{1}$

1.24
$$
\begin{aligned}
12:c &= 14:7 \\
12:c &= 2:1 \\
c \times 2 &= 12 \times 1 \\
2c &= 12 \\
\frac{2c}{2} &= \frac{12}{2} \\
c &= 6
\end{aligned}
$$

1.25
$$
\begin{aligned}
m:5 &= 25:15 \\
m:5 &= 5:3 \\
m \times 3 &= 5 \times 5 \\
3m &= 25 \\
\frac{3m}{3} &= \frac{25}{3} \\
m &= 8\tfrac{1}{3} \text{ or } 8.33
\end{aligned}
$$

1.26
$$
\begin{aligned}
9:27 &= c:3 \\
1:3 &= c:3 \\
3 \times c &= 1 \times 3 \\
3c &= 3 \\
\frac{3c}{3} &= \frac{3}{3} \\
c &= 1
\end{aligned}
$$

1.27
$$
\begin{aligned}
&\tfrac{1}{2}:f::\tfrac{3}{8}:\tfrac{11}{16} \\
f \times \frac{3}{8} &= \frac{1}{2} \times \frac{11}{16} \\
\frac{3}{8}f &= \frac{11}{32} \\
\frac{8}{3}\left(\frac{3}{8}f\right) &= \frac{8}{3}\left(\frac{11}{32}\right) \\
f &= \frac{11}{12}
\end{aligned}
$$

1.28
$$
\begin{aligned}
5 \text{ miles} &= 5 \times 5{,}280 \times 12 \\
&= 316{,}800 \text{ in.}
\end{aligned}
$$
$$
\begin{aligned}
1:25{,}000 &= d:316{,}800 \\
25{,}000 \times d &= 1 \times 316{,}800 \\
25{,}000d &= 316{,}800 \\
\frac{25{,}000d}{25{,}000} &= \frac{316{,}800}{25{,}000} \\
d &= 12.672 \\
&= 12\tfrac{2}{3}\text{" (approximately)}
\end{aligned}
$$

1.29
$$
\begin{aligned}
\frac{1}{16}:1 &= l:4\tfrac{1}{4} \\
1 \times l &= \frac{1}{16} \times 4\tfrac{1}{4} \\
l &= \frac{17}{64}\text{"}
\end{aligned}
$$

1.30 Length:
$$
\begin{aligned}
\frac{1}{4}:12 &= 4\tfrac{1}{4}:l \\
\frac{1}{4} \times l &= 12 \times 4\tfrac{1}{4} \\
\frac{1}{4}l &= 51 \\
4\left(\frac{1}{4}l\right) &= 4(51) \\
l &= 204 \text{ in.} \\
&= \frac{204}{12} \\
&= 17 \text{ ft.}
\end{aligned}
$$

Width:
$$
\begin{aligned}
\frac{1}{4}:12 &= 2\tfrac{3}{4}:w \\
\frac{1}{4} \times w &= 12 \times 2\tfrac{3}{4} \\
\frac{1}{4}w &= 33 \\
4\left(\frac{1}{4}w\right) &= 4(33) \\
w &= 132 \text{ in.} \\
&= \frac{132}{12} \\
&= 11 \text{ ft.}
\end{aligned}
$$

Actual dimensions are 17 ft. by 11 ft.

1.31

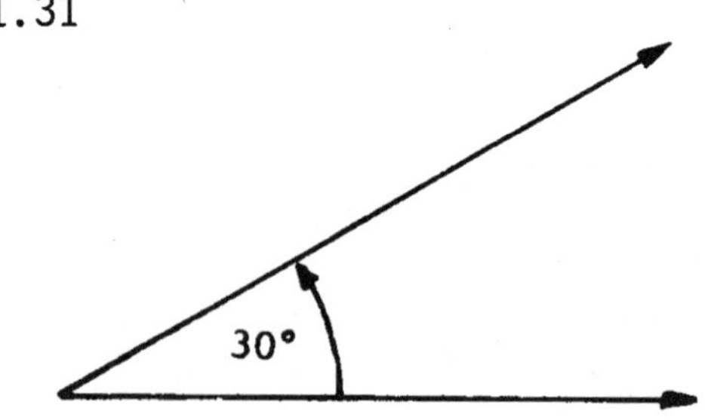

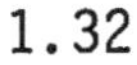
1.32

1.33 Any angle greater than 90° but less than 180°.

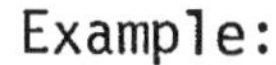
Example:

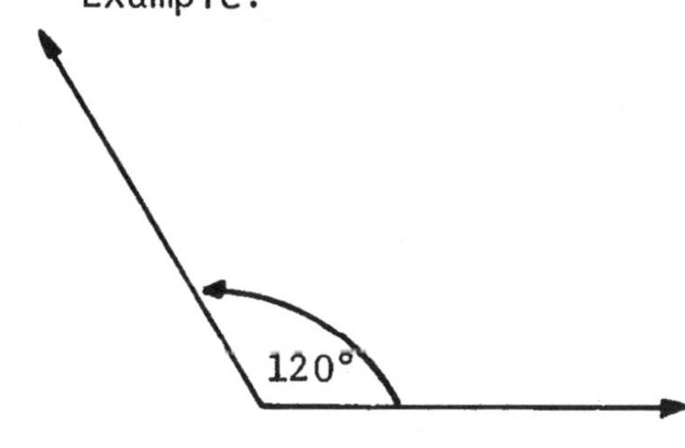

1.34

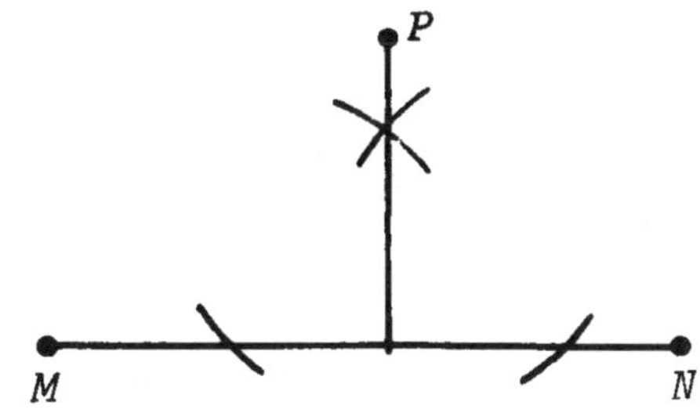

1.35 $A = 1.7205(5)^2$
$= 1.7205(25)$
$= 43.0125 \text{ in.}^2$

1.36 $A = \frac{1}{2}bh$
$= \frac{1}{2}(4)(6)$
$= 12 \text{ in.}^2$

1.37 $A = 3.634(3.5)^2$
$= 3.634(12.25)$
$= 44.5165 \text{ in.}^2$

1.38 $A = \frac{1}{2}(a + b)h$
$= \frac{1}{2}(8 + 4.5)(5.25)$
$= \frac{1}{2}(12.5)(5.25)$
$= 32.8125 \text{ in.}^2$

1.39 each interior angle =
$(1 - \frac{2}{10})180° =$
$(\frac{4}{5})180° = 144°$

1.40 sum of measures of interior angles =
$(6 - 2)180° =$
$(4)180° = 720°$

1.41 $A = \pi r^2$
$= 3.142(6)^2$
$= 3.142(36)$
$= 113.112 \text{ in.}^2$

1.42 $A = \pi ab$
$= 3.142(5.5)(3.5)$
$= 60.4835$ or 60.484 in.^2

1.43 $C = \pi d$
$= 3.142(4)$
$= 12.568 \text{ in.}^2$

1.44 $A = 2(4 \times 5 + 4 \times 6 + 5 \times 6)$
$= 2(20 + 24 + 30)$
$= 2(74)$
$= 148 \text{ in.}^2$

1.45 $V = \frac{1}{3}\pi r^2 h$
$= \frac{1}{3}(3.142)(3.5)^2(6)$
$= \frac{1}{3}(3.142)(12.25)(6)$
$= \frac{1}{3}(230.937)$
$= 76.979 \text{ in.}^3$

1.46 $V = \frac{1}{3}$(area of base times altitude)
$= \frac{1}{3}(18)(16)(20)$
$= \frac{1}{3}(5{,}760)$
$= 1{,}920 \text{ ft.}^3$

1.47 $A = 6s^2$
$= 6(8)^2$
$= 6(64)$
$= 384 \text{ in.}^2$

1.48 $A = 4\pi r^2$
$= 4(3.142)(3)^2$
$= 4(3.142)(9)$
$= 113.112 \text{ cm}^2$

1.49 5 x 3.785 = 18.925 liters

1.50 5,000 x 1.609 = 8,045 kilometers

1.51 $28.5 \times \frac{1}{28.35} =$
$\frac{28.5}{28.35} = 1.005$ ounces

1.52 55 x 1.609 = 88.495 kilometers per hour
$= \frac{88.495}{60 \times 60}$
$= \frac{88.495}{3,600}$
= 0.0246 kilometers per second

1.53 $0.0246 = 2.46 \times 10^{-2}$ kilometers per second

1.54 120 x 907.2 = 108,864 kilograms

1.55 108,864 kilograms = 108.864 megagrams

1.56 degrees Kelvin = 273 + 4,000
= 4,273°K

1.57 degrees Celsius = $\frac{5}{9}(1,800 - 32)$
$= \frac{5}{9}(1,768)$
= 982.2°C

1.58 0.005 nanoseconds =
5×10^{-3} nanoseconds or
5×10^{-12} seconds

II. SECTION TWO

2.1 40 x $2.35 = $94

2.2 Regular:
40 x $3.15 = $126

Overtime:
(8 x $3.15)(1.5) =
($25.20)(1.5) = $37.80

Weekly wage = $126 + $37.80
= $163.80

2.3 $1,500 x 12 = $18,000

2.4 $850 x 0.35 = $297.50

2.5 $2,600 - $1,150 = $1,450

2.6 b

2.7 a

2.8 b

2.9 d

2.10 a

2.11 b

2.12 f

2.13 e

2.14 Monthly payments total =
24 x $28.33 = $679.92

Total amount paid =
$60.00 + $679.92 = $739.92

Service charge =
$739.92 - $599.50 = $140.42

2.15 Monthly payments total =
12 x $46.71 = $560.52

Total amount paid =
$100.00 + $560.52 = $660.52

Service charge =
$660.52 - $575.00 = $85.52

2.16 With down payment:
Monthly payments total =
36 x $56.98 = $2,051.28

Total amount paid =
$150.00 + $2,051.28 = $2,201.28

Service charge =
$2,201.28 - $1,499.50 = $701.78

With no down payment:
Monthly payments total =
36 x $63.33 = $2,279.88

Service charge =
$2,279.88 - $1,499.50 = $780.38

Difference in service charges =
$780.38 - $701.78 = $78.60

2.17
$$\begin{aligned} I &= \frac{2(12)(875)}{4{,}200(48 + 1)} \\ &= \frac{2(12)(875)}{4{,}200(49)} \\ &= \frac{21{,}000}{205{,}800} \\ &= 0.102 \\ &= 10.2\% \end{aligned}$$

2.18
$$\begin{aligned} I &= \frac{2(12)(30{,}000)}{36{,}000(300 + 1)} \\ &= \frac{2(12)(30{,}000)}{36{,}000(301)} \\ &= \frac{720{,}000}{10{,}836{,}000} \\ &= 0.066 \\ &= 6.6\% \end{aligned}$$

2.19
$$\begin{aligned} c &= 36 \times \$28.75 - \$950 \\ &= \$1{,}035 - \$950 \\ &= \$85 \end{aligned}$$

$$\begin{aligned} I &= \frac{2(12)(85)}{950(36 + 1)} \\ &= \frac{2(12)(85)}{950(37)} \\ &= \frac{2{,}040}{35{,}150} \\ &= 0.058 \\ &= 5.8\% \end{aligned}$$

2.20 a. 0.115 x $18,000 = $2,070
b. $2,070 ÷ 12 = $172.50

2.21 a. 0.245 x $18,000 = $4,410
b. $4,410 ÷ 12 = $367.50

2.22 a. 0.095 x $18,000 = $1,710
b. $1,710 ÷ 12 = $142.50

2.23 a. 0.265 x $18,000 = $4,770
b. $4,770 ÷ 12 = $397.50

2.24 a. 0.17 x $18,000 = $3,060
b. $3,060 ÷ 12 = $255

2.25 a. 0.045 x $18,000 = $810
b. $810 ÷ 12 = $67.50

2.26 a. 0.05 x $18,000 = $900
b. $900 ÷ 12 = $75

2.27 a. 0.015 x $18,000 = $270
b. $270 ÷ 12 = $22.50

2.28
$$\begin{array}{r} \$415.13 \\ +\ 158.14 \\ \hline \$573.27 \\ -\ 500.25 \\ \hline \$\ 73.02 \end{array}$$

2.29
$$\begin{array}{r} \$1{,}012.15 \\ +\ \ 515.30 \\ \hline \$1{,}527.45 \\ -\ \ 965.38 \\ \hline \$\ \ 562.07 \\ -\ \ \ \ 5.55 \\ \hline \$\ \ 556.52 \end{array}$$

2.30 6

2.31 2

2.32 $538.65 + $49.19 = $587.84

2.33 $400.00 + $158.00 = $558.00

2.34 $49.19 + $68.28 + $199.39 + $215.58 + $425.00 + $83.26 = $1,040.70

2.35 $2.50

2.36 $102.64

III. SECTION THREE

3.1 true

3.2 false

3.3 true

3.4 true

Average rate for luxury automobile $= \frac{\$98 + \$84 + \$60}{3}$

$= \frac{\$242}{3}$

$= \$80.67$

Average rate for compact automobile $= \frac{\$26 + \$22 + \$16}{3}$

$= \frac{\$64}{3}$

$= \$21.33$

$\frac{\$80.67}{\$21.33} = 3.8$, which is almost 4

3.5 false

3.6 $I = \$6{,}500 \times 0.055 \times 8$

$= \$2{,}860$

3.7 Find in the chart the amount of $1.00 at 2% for 60 years and multiply by $8,500:
3.2810308 x $8,500 = $27,888.76

3.8 $I = \$1{,}000 \times 0.06 \times \frac{90}{360}$

$= \$1{,}000 \times 0.06 \times 0.25$

$= \$15$

3.9 Apply the $100 exemption to the chinaware. The amount of $250 remains to be figured at the prevailing duty rate.

Duty on camera = $155(0.15)
= $23.25

Duty on pearls = $85(0.55)
= $46.75

3.9 cont.

Duty on chinaware = $250(0.35)
= $87.50

Total amount of duty = $23.25 + $46.75 + $87.50
= $157.50

3.10 a. Since the shirts are valued at less than $10 each, no duty is levied on them.

Duty on sweater = $39.50(0.2)
= $7.90

Duty on suitcases (after applying the $100 exemption) = $27.50(0.2)
= $5.50

Total amount of duty = $7.90 + $5.50
= $13.40

b. $440.80(0.52) = $229.22

3.11 depreciated

3.12 $\frac{0.1601 - 0.1190}{0.1601} = \frac{0.0411}{0.1601}$

$= 0.257$

$= 25.7\%$

3.13 e

3.14 a

3.15 f

3.16 c

3.17 d

3.18 a. Total costs = Fixed costs + Variable costs
= $1,000 + $0.40(2,500)
= $1,000 + $1,000
= $2,000

b. Profit = Revenue - Total costs
= $1.49(2,250) - $2,000
= $3,352.50 - $2,000
= $1,352.50

3.19 $\$670 - \$670(0.03) = \$670 - \$20.10 = \$649.90$

3.20 Area of garage = 180 x 175
= 31,500 ft.^{2}

Space available for parking = $\frac{31,500}{2}$
= 15,750 ft.^{2}

Number of cars = $\frac{15,750}{250} \times 4$
= 63 x 4
= 252

3.21 Time spent making out reports = $\frac{1}{8} \times 40$
= 5 hours

Time spent at guard headquarters = $\frac{1}{16} \times 40$
= $2\frac{1}{2}$ hours

Time spent on patrol = $40 - (5 + 2\frac{1}{2})$
= $40 - 7\frac{1}{2}$
= $32\frac{1}{2}$ hours

3.22 Labor cost = \$12.75 x 2.5
= \$31.88

Overhead cost = \$31.88 x 0.8
= \$25.50

Total charges = \$31.88 + \$25.50
= \$57.38

3.23 $V = 30 \times 15 \times 4.5$
= 2,025 ft.^{3}

Number of gallons = 2,025 x 7.5
= 15,187.5 gallons

3.24 $\frac{15,187.5}{1,400} = 10.85$ = 10 hours and 51 minutes

3.25 $V = \pi r^2 h$

$V = 3.142(\frac{9}{32}")^2 (180")$

= 44.74 in.^{3}

$= \frac{44.74}{12 \times 12 \times 12}$

$= \frac{44.74}{1,728}$

= 0.026 ft.^{3}

3.25 cont.

Weight of rod:
$1:485 = 0.026:w$
$1 \times w = 485 \times 0.026$
w = 12.6 pounds (approximately)

3.26 $V = 1,980 \times 15 \times 10$
= 297,000 in.^{3}

$= \frac{297,000}{12 \times 12 \times 12}$

$= \frac{297,000}{1,728}$

= 171.875 or 171.88 ft.^{3}

3.27 false

3.28 true

3.29 false

3.30 true

3.31 c

3.32 a

3.33 b

CONSUMER MATHEMATICS 1
SELF TEST
SOLUTION KEY

SELF TEST 1

1.01 278

1.02 238

1.03 309

1.04 2,278

1.05 1,734

1.06 385

1.07 455

1.08 184

1.09 1,212

1.010 1,317

1.011 185

1.012 426

1.013
```
   64
   49
  576
 256
 3,136
```

1.014 2,862

1.015
```
   574
    31
   574
 1722
 17,794
```

1.016 308

1.017 184

1.018
```
   56
   82
  112
 448
 4,592
```

1.019 3,730

1.020
```
   602
   145
  3010
 2408
 602
 87,290
```

1.021 168

1.022 2,922

1.023
```
   57
   29
  513
 114
 1,653
```

1.024
```
   45
   72
   90
 315
 3,240
```

1.025
```
    809
     65
   4045
  4854
  52,585
```

1.026
```
     99 R2
 4)398
   36
    38
    36
     2
```

1.027
```
      2 R5
 44)93
    88
     5
```

1.028
```
       5
 75)375
    375
      0
```

1.029
```
      26 R19
 24)643
    48
    163
    144
     19
```

1.030
```
   107 R1
 5)536
   5
   036
    35
     1
```

1.031
```
     6 R1
13)79
   78
    1
```

1.032
```
     6 R32
81)518
   486
    32
```

1.033
```
    11 R8
19)217
   19
    27
    19
     8
```

1.034
```
   41 R5
9)374
  36
   14
    9
    5
```

1.035
```
    23 R16
32)752
   64
   112
    96
    16
```

SELF TEST 2

2.01 The largest one-digit number divisible by 5 is 5; therefore, the first digit must be 1 since 5 divided by 5 is 1. The third digit is 5. Three plus 5 equals 8, so 3 is the second number. Since the first digit is 1, 3 must be the second number (the difference of 3 and 1 is 2).

2.01 (continued)

Therefore, R = 135.

a. 1
b. 3
c. 5

2.02 The third digit must be either 1 or 2.

The first digit must be either 4 or 8 (4 x 1 = 4; 4 x 2 = 8).

The second digit must be either 3 or 6 (3 x 1 = 3; 3 x 2 = 6).

For the digits to add to 16, they must be 8, 6, and 2.

Therefore, Y = 862.

a. 8
b. 6
c. 2

2.03 Since the first and third digits are odd, they must be 1, 3, 5, 7, or 9.

Since the second and fourth digits are even, they must be 2, 4, 6, or 8.

For the fourth digit to be two times the first digit, the fourth digit must be either 2 or 6 (2 x 1 = 2; 2 x 3 = 6).

For the first and second digits to add to seven, the second digit must be 6 or 4 (1 + 6 = 7 3 + 4 = 7).

2.03 cont.

For the second and third digits to add to nine, the third digit must be 3 or 5 (6 + 3 = 9; 4 + 5 = 9).

For the third and fourth digits to add to eleven, the third digit must be 5 and the fourth digit must be 6. Therefore, the first digit must be 3 and the second digit must be 4.

Therefore, Q = 3,456.
a. 3 c. 5
b. 4 d. 6

2.04 Since the digits are all the same and they add to 16, each digit must be 4 (16 ÷ 4 = 4). Also, 4 x 4 = 16.

Therefore, F = 4,444.
a. 4
b. 4
c. 4
d. 4

2.05 The factors of 35 are 1, 5, 7, and 35, of which 7 is the largest prime factor. Therefore, the first digit is 7.

The factors of 24 are 1, 2, 3, 4, 6, 8, 12, and 24, of which 2 is the smallest prime factor. Therefore, the third digit is 2.

Since the last digit plus the first digit add to 12, the last digit must be 12 minus the first digit, or 12 minus 7, which equals 5.

The factors of 110 are 1, 2, 5, 10, 11, 22, 55, and 110, of which 5 is the second largest prime number.

Therefore, Z = 7,525.
a. 7
b. 5
c. 2
d. 5

SELF TEST 3

3.01 a. 9 x 7 = 63
b. 63 x 2 x 2 = 252

3.02 3,323 + 1,621 = 4,944
8,474 - 4,944 = 3,530

3.03 234 - 186 = 48

3.04
```
     287 R16
17)4895
   34
   149
   136
    135
    119
     16
```

3.05
```
  183
 x 27
 1281
 366
 4941
```

3.06 22 ÷ 2 = 11 horses
11 x 3 = 33 water bottles

3.07 a. 5 x 47 = 235
b. 235 x 9 = 2,115

3.08 2,242 ÷ 118 = 19

3.09 9 x 23 = 207

3.010 a. 12 pencils = 2 x 2 = 4 rulers
4 rulers = 4 x 2 = 8 erasers
b. 2 erasers = 1 ruler
1 ruler = 6 ÷ 2 = 3 pencils
c. 1 ruler = 6 ÷ 2 = 3 pencils
4 erasers = 4 ÷ 2 = 2 rulers
2 rulers = 6 pencils
3 + 6 = 9 pencils

3.011 The factors of 35 are 1, 5, 7, and 35. The prime factors are 5 and 7, of which 7 is the largest.

3.012 The factors of 38 are 1, 2, 19, and 38. The prime factors are 2 and 19, of which 19 is the largest.

3.013 2

3.014 The factors of 12 are 1, 2, 3, 4, 6, and 12. The prime factors are 2 and 3, of which 2 is the smallest.

3.015 3

CONSUMER MATHEMATICS 2
SELF TEST
SOLUTION KEY

SELF TEST 1

1.01 $\frac{17}{2} \times \frac{7}{2} = \frac{119}{4}$

1.02 $\frac{1}{16} \times \frac{4}{3} = \frac{4}{48} = \frac{1}{12}$

1.03 $\frac{32}{12} + \frac{9}{12} = \frac{41}{12}$

1.04 $\frac{20}{24} - \frac{3}{24} = \frac{17}{24}$

1.05 $\frac{25}{4} \div \frac{7}{3} = \frac{25}{4} \times \frac{3}{7} = \frac{75}{28}$

1.06 $\frac{8}{7} \times \frac{13}{6} = \frac{104}{42} = \frac{52}{21}$

1.07 $\frac{14}{1} \times \frac{7}{3} = \frac{98}{3}$

1.08 $\frac{27}{15} - \frac{20}{15} = \frac{7}{15}$

1.09 $\frac{5}{2} + \frac{17}{16} = \frac{40}{16} + \frac{17}{16} = \frac{57}{16}$

1.010 $\frac{9}{32}$

1.011 $\frac{12}{9} + \frac{1}{9} = \frac{13}{9}$

1.012 $\frac{1}{2} \div \frac{22}{3} = \frac{1}{2} \times \frac{3}{22} = \frac{3}{44}$

1.013 $\frac{12}{20} + \frac{15}{20} = \frac{27}{20}$

1.014 $\frac{10}{7} - \frac{4}{5} = \frac{50}{35} - \frac{28}{35} = \frac{22}{35}$

1.015 $\frac{14}{15} - \frac{5}{15} = \frac{9}{15} = \frac{3}{5}$

1.016 $\frac{36}{44} + \frac{33}{44} = \frac{69}{44}$

1.017 $\frac{4}{16} = \frac{1}{4}$

1.018 $\frac{13}{2} \div \frac{4}{1} = \frac{13}{2} \times \frac{1}{4} = \frac{13}{8}$

1.019 $\frac{25}{8} - \frac{13}{6} = \frac{75}{24} - \frac{52}{24} = \frac{23}{24}$

1.020 $\frac{4}{10} \times \frac{3}{1} = \frac{12}{10} = \frac{6}{5}$

1.021 $\frac{15}{5} = 3$

1.022 $\frac{18}{30} - \frac{10}{30} = \frac{8}{30} = \frac{4}{15}$

1.023 $\frac{1}{3} \times \frac{4}{1} = \frac{4}{3}$

1.024 $\frac{25}{8} \times \frac{7}{16} = \frac{175}{128}$

1.025 $\frac{11}{12}$

1.026 $\frac{7}{9} + \frac{3}{2} = \frac{14}{18} + \frac{27}{18} = \frac{41}{18}$

1.027 $640 \div \frac{1}{2} = 640 \times \frac{2}{1} = 1{,}280$ plots

1.028 $\frac{1}{8} \times 2\frac{1}{6} = \frac{1}{8} \times \frac{13}{6} = \frac{13}{48}$ quart

1.029 $10\frac{1}{2} + 6\frac{1}{3} = \frac{21}{2} + \frac{19}{3} = \frac{63}{6} +$
$\frac{38}{6} = \frac{101}{6}$ dozen

1.030 $8\frac{1}{4} \times 5 = \frac{33}{4} \times \frac{5}{1} = \frac{165}{4}$ cents

1.031 $47\frac{1}{2} \div 50\frac{1}{3} = \frac{95}{2} \div \frac{151}{3} =$
$\frac{95}{2} \times \frac{3}{151} = \frac{285}{302}$ hour

1.032 $3\frac{1}{4} + 2\frac{1}{2} = \frac{13}{4} + \frac{5}{2} = \frac{13}{4} + \frac{10}{4} =$
$\frac{23}{4}$ hours

1.033 $12\frac{1}{4} - 3\frac{1}{3} = \frac{49}{4} - \frac{10}{3} = \frac{147}{12} -$
$\frac{40}{12} = \frac{107}{12}$ yards

1.034 $\frac{3}{8} \times \frac{1}{4} = \frac{3}{32}$

1.035 $16\frac{3}{8} \div 9 = \frac{131}{8} \div \frac{9}{1} =$
$\frac{131}{8} \times \frac{1}{9} = \frac{131}{72}$ feet

1.036 Example:
a number with a horizontal bar, a whole number above the bar, and a whole number below the bar

1.037 Example:
the number above the bar in a fraction

1.038 Example:
the number below the bar in a fraction

1.039 Example:
a fraction less than 1

1.040 Example:
a fraction greater than 1

1.041 Example:
a number containing a whole number part and a fraction part

1.042 Example:
fractions with the same numerical value

1.043 Example:
a number into which two denominators will both divide evenly

1.044 Example:
put the numerator below the bar and the denominator above it

1.045 Any order:
a. a part of a whole
b. a division
c. a ratio

SELF TEST 2

2.01 improper

2.02 mixed

2.03 1

2.04 proper

2.05 improper

2.06 mixed

2.07 $\frac{4}{12} + \frac{9}{12} = \frac{13}{12}$

2.08
```
      .2581 = 0.258
  16)4.1310
     32
      93
      80
      131
      128
        30
        16
```

2.09 $\frac{16}{45}$

2.010
```
   43.7
    0.042
 + 68
 111.742
```

2.011 $\frac{1}{16} \times \frac{4}{3} = \frac{4}{48} = \frac{1}{12}$

2.012 $\frac{2}{4} = \frac{1}{2}$

2.013
```
  143.600
 -  0.414
  143.186
```

2.014 $\frac{13}{2} + \frac{8}{7} = \frac{91}{14} + \frac{16}{14} = \frac{107}{14}$

2.015 347.21

2.016
47.3
x 0.012
946
473
0.5676 = 0.568

2.017
33.7062 = 33.706
143)4820.0000
429
530
429
1010
1001
900
858
420
286

2.018 Example:
of two fractions, a number into which both denominators will divide evenly

2.019 Example:
a fraction with a numerical value less than 1

2.020 Example:
based on ten

2.021 Example:
such that the only common factor of numerator and denominator is 1

2.022 Example:
a number less than 1 written with a decimal point and place values

2.023
76,421
x 0.04
3.05684 inches

2.024 $\frac{1}{9} \times \frac{3}{8} = \frac{3}{72} = \frac{1}{24}$

2.025
10.5
x 4.7
735
420
49.35¢ or $0.49

2.026
19.479 = $19.48
843)16421.400
843
7991
7587
4044
3372
6720
5901
8190
7587

2.027 70 meters = 231 feet;
1 kilometer = 1,000 meters;
70 kilometers = 231,000 feet

2.028 $11\frac{1}{8}$ = 11.125
577.4382 = 577.438 mph
11.125)6424.0000000
55625
86150
77875
82750
77875
48750
44500
42500
33375
91250
89000
22500
22250

2.029
3.19
x 4.6
1914
1276
14.674
x 2.7
102718
29348
39.6198 = 39.620 cubic units

2.030 $\begin{array}{r} \$13.50 \\ \times \quad 24 \\ \hline 5400 \\ 2700 \\ \hline \$324.00 \end{array}$ = $324

2.031 $7\frac{1}{4} \div 11 = \frac{29}{4} \div \frac{11}{1} =$

$\frac{29}{4} \times \frac{1}{11} = \frac{29}{44}$ yard

or

7.25 ÷ 11 =

$$\begin{array}{r} 0.6590 \\ 11\overline{)7.250} \\ \underline{66} \\ 65 \\ \underline{55} \\ 100 \\ \underline{99} \\ 10 \end{array}$$ = 0.659 yard

2.032 $\begin{array}{r} \$1.75 \\ \times \quad 3.5 \\ \hline 875 \\ 525 \\ \hline 6.125 \end{array}$ = $6.13

SELF TEST 3

3.01 Example:
a symbol consisting of a bar, a whole number above the bar, and a whole number other than zero below the bar

3.02 Example:
a number with a value less than 1 written with a decimal point

3.03 Example:
the number above the bar in a fraction

3.04 Example:
the number below the bar in a fraction

3.05 Example:
a number with a whole number part and a fraction part

3.06 Example:
per hundred

3.07 Example:
a fraction with a value greater than 1

3.08 a. 25%
b. 0.25

3.09 a. 44.4%
b. 0.444

3.010 a. $\frac{45}{100} = 0.45$
b. $\frac{45}{100} = \frac{9}{20}$

3.011 a. 140%
b. $1\frac{4}{10} = 1\frac{2}{5}$ or $\frac{7}{5}$

3.012 a. 62.5%
b. $\frac{625}{1,000} = \frac{5}{8}$

3.013 a. 0.5
b. $\frac{50}{100} = \frac{1}{2}$

3.014 $\frac{3}{4} + \frac{7}{8} = \frac{6}{8} + \frac{7}{8} = \frac{13}{8}$ hours

3.015 103 x 0.91 = 93.73 = 94 people

3.016 1 kilogram = 1,000 grams
3 kilograms = 3,000 grams;
3 kilograms = 6.618 pounds;
3 grams = 0.006618 pound

3.017 $14,200 x 0.57 = $8,094

3.018 $4\frac{1}{4} + 3\frac{1}{8} = \frac{17}{4} + \frac{25}{8} = \frac{34}{8} +$
$\frac{25}{8} = \frac{59}{8}$ cups

3.019 1,000 ÷ 3.15 = 317.46 bushels

3.020 421 x $0.59 = $248.39

3.021 $91.50 x 0.10 = $9.15

3.022 79 ÷ 424 = 0.186 = 18.6%

3.023 $4 \times \frac{1}{8} = \frac{4}{8} = \frac{1}{2}$ of the cake

3.024 37 x 0.84 = 31.08 = 31 men

3.025 $642 x 0.14 = $89.88

3.026 403 ÷ 0.29 = 1,389.655

3.027 14 ÷ 1,043 = 0.0134 = 1.34%

3.028 14 x 0.83 = 11.62

3.029 51 ÷ 63 = 0.8095 = 80.95%

3.030 296 ÷ 0.58 = 510.345

CONSUMER MATHEMATICS 3
SELF TEST
SOLUTION KEY

SELF TEST 1

1.01 $12,000 ÷ 24 = $500

1.02 $16,500 ÷ 52 = $317.31

1.03 $27,050 ÷ 12 = $2,254.17

1.04 $14,500 ÷ 26 = $557.69

1.05 $475.25 x 26 = $12,356.50

1.06 $1,937 x 12 = $23,244

1.07 $875 x 24 = $21,000

1.08 $1,000 x 52 = $52,000

1.09
a. 40
b. 40
c. 40 x $3.85 = $154.00

1.010
a. $39\frac{1}{2}$
b. $39\frac{1}{2}$
c. $39\frac{1}{2}$ x $4.00 =
39.5 x $4.00 = $158.00

1.011
a. $37\frac{1}{2}$
b. $37\frac{1}{2}$
c. $37\frac{1}{2}$ x $3.50 =
37.5 x $3.50 = $131.25

1.012
a. 45
b. 45 - 40 = 5 overtime hours
$45 + (\frac{1}{2} \times 5) = 45 + 2\frac{1}{2} = 47\frac{1}{2}$
c. $47\frac{1}{2}$ x $4.10 = 47.5 x $4.10 =
$194.75

1.013
a. $44\frac{1}{2}$
b. $44\frac{1}{2} - 40 = 4\frac{1}{2}$ overtime hours
$44\frac{1}{2} + (\frac{1}{2} \times 4\frac{1}{2}) = 44\frac{1}{2} +$
$(\frac{1}{2} \times \frac{9}{2}) = 44\frac{1}{2} + \frac{9}{4} = 46\frac{3}{4}$
c. $46\frac{3}{4}$ x $3.00 = 46.75 x $3.00 =
$140.25

1.014
a. 54
b. 54 x $2.13 = $115.02

1.015
a. 659
b. 659 x $0.17 = $112.03

1.016 0.15 x $425 = $63.75
$63.75 + $145 = $208.75

1.017
a. 0.275 x $1,200 = $330
b. 0.275 x $675 = $185.63
c. 0.275 x $1,900 = $522.50
d. 0.275 x $1,000 = $275
e. 0.275 x $400 = $110
f. 0.275 x $930 = $255.75

1.018 $37,500 - $45,000 = ($7,500)

1.019 $98,000 + $25,000 = $123,000 expenses
$147,000 - $123,000 = $24,000

SELF TEST 2

2.01 money paid an employee by the day, week, month, or year, but not by the hours worked or the units produced

2.02 money paid to a worker by the hours worked or by the units produced

2.03 twice a month

2.04 every two weeks

2.05 a percentage of sales paid to salesmen as wages

2.06 0.0325 x $27,500 = $893.75

2.07 $\frac{27,000}{1,173,913} = 0.023 = 2.3\%$

2.08 $89.95 + $257.00 = $346.95
0.05 x $346.95 = $17.35

2.09 a. 41
b. 41 - 40 = 1 overtime hour
$41 + (\frac{1}{2} \times 1) = 41 + \frac{1}{2} = 41\frac{1}{2}$
c. $41\frac{1}{2}$ x $4.75 = 41.5 x $4.75 = $197.13
d. 0.0605 x $197.13 = $11.93
e. $29.80 (from the table)
f. 0.03 x $197.13 = $5.91
g. 0.011 x $197.13 = $2.17
h. $11.93 + $29.80 + $5.91 + $2.17 = $49.81
i. $197.13 - $49.81 = $147.32

2.010 a. 4,380
b. $0.05 x 4,380 = $219.00
c. 0.0605 x $219 = $13.25
d. $37.10 (from the table)
e. 0.028 x $219 = $6.13
f. $13.25 + $37.10 + $6.13 = $56.48
g. $219.00 - $56.48 = $162.52

2.011 a. 0.375 x $485 = $181.88
b. 0.0605 x $181.88 = $11.00
c. $24.70 (from the table)
d. 0.015 x $181.88 = $2.73
e. 0.032 x $181.88 = $5.82
f. $11.00 + $24.70 + $2.73 + $5.82 = $44.25
g. $181.88 - $44.25 = $137.63

2.012 $12,000 ÷ 52 = $230.77

2.013 $525 x 26 = $13,650

2.014 $19,500 ÷ 24 = $812.50

2.015 $1,375 x 12 = $16,500

2.016 Total expenses: $45,750
$53,000 - $45,750 = $7,250

SELF TEST 3

3.01 a. 0.11 x $12,000 = $1,320
b. $1,320 ÷ 12 = $110

3.02 a. $0.\overline{3}$ x $12,000 = $4,000
b. $4,000 ÷ 12 = $333.33

3.03 a. 0.07 x $12,000 = $840
b. $840 ÷ 12 = $70

3.04 a. $0.0\overline{6}$ (or 0.067)x $12,000 = $800
b. $800 ÷ 12 = $66.67

3.05 a. 0.14 x $12,000 = $1,680
b. $1,680 ÷ 12 = $140

3.06 a. 0.05 x $12,000 = $600
b. $600 ÷ 12 = $50

3.07 a. 0.07 x $12,000 = $840
b. $840 ÷ 12 = $70

3.08 a. 0.095 x $12,000 = $1,140
b. $1,140 ÷ 12 = $95

3.09 a. 0.065 x $12,000 = $780
b. $780 ÷ 12 = $65

3.010 $32 ÷ $320 = 0.1 = 10%

3.011 $76 ÷ $320 = 0.2375 = 23.75%

3.012 $80 ÷ $320 = 0.25 = 25%

3.013 $52 ÷ $320 = 0.1625 = 16.25%

3.014 $32 ÷ $320 = 0.1 = 10%

3.015 $16 ÷ $320 = 0.05 = 5%

3.016 $32 ÷ $320 = 0.1 = 10%

3.017 Total expenses: $166,500.00
$183,000.00 - $166,500.00 = $16,500

3.018 $230.77 x 52 = $12,000.04 or $12,000

3.019 $16,500 ÷ 12 = $1,375

3.020 $812.50 x 24 = $19,500

3.021 50 - 40 = 10 overtime hours
$50 + (\frac{1}{2} \times 10) = 50 + 5 =$ 55 paid hours
55 x $2.90 = $159.50

3.022 $0.12 x 5,321 = $638.52

3.023 $0.283 \times \$631 = \$178.57$

3.024 $32.90

3.025 $22.60

3.026 $27.50

3.027 $0.0605 \times \$212.13 = \$12.83$

3.028 $0.0605 \times \$87.50 = \$5.29$

SELF TEST 4

4.01 $3 \times \$7.00 = \$21.00$
$\$175.00 + \$19.98 + \$21.00 = \$215.98$
$\$215.98 \times 0.07 = \$15.12$

4.02 $\frac{9,500,000}{340,000,000} = 0.028 = 2.8\%$

4.03 $\$12,000 \times 0.028 = \$336$

4.04 $0.25 \times \$738 = \$184.50$

4.05 $0.135 \times \$648 = \$87.48$

4.06 $0.148 \times \$1,048 = \$155.10$

4.07 $\$16,000 \div 52 = \$307.69$

4.08 $\$557.69 \times 26 = \$14,499.94$

4.09 $\$625.00 \times 24 = \$15,000$

4.010 $\$14,400 \div 12 = \$1,200$

4.011 a. 371
b. $371 \times \$0.27 = \$100.17$

4.012 a. 679
b. $679 \times 15¢ = \$101.85$

4.013 a. $37\frac{1}{2}$
b. $37\frac{1}{2}$
c. $37\frac{1}{2} \times \$3.50 = 37.5 \times \$3.50 = \$131.25$

4.014 a. 45
b. $45 - 40 = 5$ overtime hours
$45 + (\frac{1}{2} \times 5) = 45 + 2\frac{1}{2} = 47\frac{1}{2}$
c. $47\frac{1}{2} \times \$4.10 = 47.5 \times \$4.10 = \$194.75$

4.015 a. $44\frac{1}{2}$
b. $44\frac{1}{2} - 40 = 4\frac{1}{2}$ overtime hours
$44\frac{1}{2} + (\frac{1}{2} \times 4\frac{1}{2}) = 44\frac{1}{2} + (\frac{1}{2} \times \frac{9}{2}) = 44\frac{1}{2} + \frac{9}{4} = 46\frac{3}{4}$
c. $46\frac{3}{4} \times \$3.10 = 46.75 \times \$3.10 = \$144.93$

4.016 $\$1,620 \div \$13,500 = 0.12 = 12\%$

4.017 $0.12 \times \$13,500 = \$1,620$

4.018 $0.26 \times \$13,500 = \$3,510$

4.019 $0.20 \times \$13,500 = \$2,700$

4.020 $\$1,350 \div \$13,500 = 0.1 = 10\%$

4.021 $0.03 \times \$13,500 = \$405$

4.022 $0.04 \times \$13,500 = \$540$

4.023 $\$675 \div \$13,500 = 0.05 = 5\%$

4.024 $0.08 \times \$13,500 = \$1,080$

4.025 Any order:
a. Tithe first.
b. Let God lead.
c. Determine fixed expenses.
d. Estimate other expenses.
e. Plan a realistic budget.
f. Divide your paycheck by the budget.
g. Do not spend money you do not have.

4.026 Any order:
a. Make a list.
b. Use cents-off coupons.
c. Compare prices.

4.027 a. $\$67.50 - \$47.50 = \$20.00$
b. $\$20.00 \div \$47.50 = 0.421 = 42.1\%$
c. $\$20.00 \div \$67.50 = 0.296 = 29.6\%$

4.028 a. $175.00 + $100.00 = $275.00
b. $100 ÷ $175 = 0.571 = 57.1%
c. $100 ÷ $275 = 0.364 =
36.4%

4.029 a. $1,000.00 - $427.41 =
$572.59
b. $427.41 ÷ $572.59 = 0.746 =
74.6%
c. $427.41 ÷ $1,000.00 = 0.427
42.7%

4.030 Note: figure (b) first.
a. $67.50 - $10.13 = $57.37
b. $67.50 x 0.15 = $10.13
c. $10.13 ÷ $57.37 = 0.177 =
17.7%

4.031 a. $190.00 x 0.65 = $123.50
b. $190.00 + $123.50 = $313.50
c. $123.50 ÷ $313.50 = 0.394 =
39.4%

4.032 a. $1.79 ÷ 4 = $0.4475
b. $2.99 ÷ 8 = $0.3738
c. b

4.033 a. $4.19 ÷ 100 = $0.0419
b. $1.60 ÷ 39 = $0.0410
c. b

4.034 a. 99¢ ÷ 5 = 19.8¢ a can
19.8¢ ÷ 6½ = 19.8¢ ÷ 6.5 =
3.0¢
b. 19¢ ÷ 6 = 3.2¢
c. a

4.035 a. $129 x 30 = $3,870
$3,870 + $499 = $4,369
b. $4,369 - $3,069 = $1,300

4.036 a. $25 x 12 = $300
$300 + $25 = $325
b. $325 - $249 = $76

4.037 a. $100 x 30 = $3,000
$3,000 + $100 = $3,100
b. $3,100 - $2,500 = $600

CONSUMER MATHEMATICS 4
SELF TEST
SOLUTION KEY

SELF TEST 1

1.01 limited-payment life

1.02 term

1.03 ordinary whole-life

1.04 endowment

1.05 a. $18.60 x 10 = $186.00
b. 0.26 x $186.00 = $48.36

1.06 a. $24.73 x 25 = $618.25
b. 0.51 x $618.25 = $315.31

1.07 a. Find the premium for a person aged 22 (25 - 3 = 22) under the "10-Year Term" column: $4.06.
$4.06 x 15 = $60.90
b. 0.09 x $60.90 = $5.48

1.08 a. Find the premium for a person aged 34 (37 - 3 = 34) under the "20-Year Endowment" column: $43.64.
$43.64 x 12 = $523.68
b. 0.26 x $523.68 = $136.16

1.09 24 - 3 = 21

1.010 43

1.011 Harold's car belongs to Class 2B.
$917.90 + $180.00 = $1,097.90

1.012 The insurance company will pay all of Mr. Bland's medical costs since $8,000 is less than the $50,000 coverage; $50,000 of Mrs. Bland's medical costs; and all of the medical costs for Bland's daughter. The insurance company will pay $8,000 + $50,000 + $20,000 = $78,000.

1.013 Harold White

1.014 $106 (use Figure 4)

1.015 2.00 x $875 = $1,750

1.016 Any five of these seven examples:
a. life
b. automobile
c. homeowners'
d. liability
e. fire
hospitalization
malpractice

SELF TEST 2

2.01

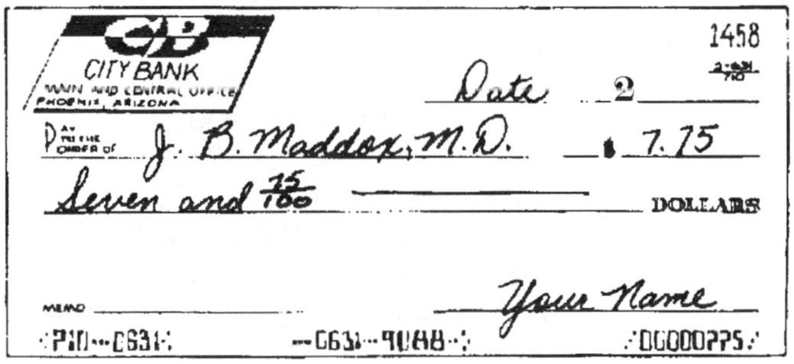

CITY BANK
MAIN AND CENTRAL OFFICE
PHOENIX, ARIZONA
1458
Date 2
PAY TO THE ORDER OF J. B. Maddox, M.D. $ 7.75
Seven and 75/100 DOLLARS
MEMO
Your Name

2.02

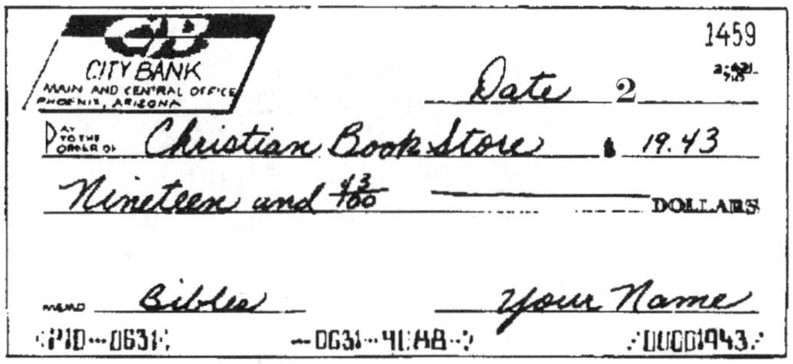

CITY BANK
MAIN AND CENTRAL OFFICE
PHOENIX, ARIZONA
1459
Date 2
PAY TO THE ORDER OF Christian Book Store $ 19.43
Nineteen and 43/100 DOLLARS
MEMO Bibles
Your Name

2.03

CHECK NO	DATE	CHECKS ISSUED TO OR DESCRIPTION OF DEPOSIT	AMOUNT OF CHECK		AMOUNT OF DEPOSIT		BALANCE FORWARD		
								1,034	27
5734		To Luphe's Market	78	21			Check or Dep	78	21
		For food					Bal	956	06
		To DEPOSIT			431	80	Check or Dep	431	80
		For PAYCHECK					Bal	1,387	86
5735		To Broadmoor Comm. Church	43	18			Check or Dep	43	18
		For tithe					Bal	1,344	68
5736		To Bill Baughman	50	00			Check or Dep	50	00
		For plumbing service					Bal	1,294	68
		To					Check or Dep		
		For					Bal		
		To					Check or Dep		
		For					Bal		

2.04 a. 3
b. 5
c. 2
d. 1
e. 4

2.05 a. Find in Figure 8 the amount of $1.00 at 6% for 25 years and multiply by $6,500:
4.2918707 x $6,500 = $27,897.16
b. $27,897.16 - $6,500 = $21,397.16
c. Find in the chart the amount of $1.00 at 3% for 50 years and multiply by $6,500:
4.3839060 x $6,500 = $28,495.39
d. $28,495.39 - $6,500 = $21,995.39
e. Find in the chart the amount of $1.00 at 1½% for 100 years and multiply by $6,500:
4.4320457 x $6,500 = $28,808.30
f. $28,808.30 - $6,500 = $22,308.30

2.06 Any three of these five examples:
a. safety deposit box
b. cashier's or certified check
c. traveler's checks
currency exchange
financial counseling

2.07 48

2.08 a. $33.14 x 30 = $994.20
b. 0.51 x $994.20 = $507.04
c. 0.26 x $994.20 = $258.49
d. 0.09 x $994.20 = $89.48

2.09 d

2.010 c

2.011 f

2.012 e

2.013 g

2.014 h

2.015 b

2.016 i

2.017 a

SELF TEST 3

3.01 through 3.05. Any order:

3.01 He can neglect to make a will, in which case the law will dispose of his estate.

3.02 He can put all his property into joint ownership; that is, he can provide that he and his wife own all his property jointly.

3.03 He can make a will that distributes outright all of his estate to one or several named persons or institutions.

3.04 He can make a will leaving his estate in trust.

3.05 He can dispose of his estate while he is still living by placing it in a living trust or by giving it away.

3.06 Teacher check:
ideas should include responsibility to provide for family members and responsibility to serve God with possessions even after death.

3.07 Find the premium for a person aged 31 (34 - 3 = 31) under the "20-Payment Life" column: $24.75.
$24.75 x 40 = $990.00

3.08 $317.80

3.09 $90

3.010 $81.80 x 250% =
$81.80 x 2.50 = $204.50

3.011 $42.01 x 20 = $840.20

3.012 Abe is 48 years old for insurance purposes.
$30.50 x 35 = $1,067.50

3.013 Any three of these five examples:
a. homeowners'
b. liability
c. fire
hospitalization
malpractice

3.014 Add the outstanding checks:
$30.90 + $17.50 + $98.10 =
$146.50
Subtract from the ending balance: $378.19 -
$146.50 = $231.69
Add the deposit:
$231.69 + $309.00 = $540.69
Subtract the service charge from the balance in the record book:
$544.90 - $4.21 = $540.69
No, an error does not exist.

3.015 a. Find in Figure 8 the amount of $1.00 at 6% for 20 years and multiply by $150:
3.2071355 x $150 =
$481.07
b. $481.07 - $150 = $331.07
c. Find in the chart the amount of $1.00 at 3% for 40 years and multiply by $150:
3.2620378 x $150 =
$489.31
d. $489.31 - $150 = $339.31
e. Find in the chart the amount of $1.00 at $1\frac{1}{2}$% for 80 years and multiply by $150:
3.2906628 x $150 =
$493.60
f. $493.60 - $150 = $343.60

3.016 $\$1{,}000 \times 0.075 \times \frac{280}{360} =$
$1,000 x 0.075 x 0.77778 =
$58.33

3.017 $480,000 ÷ 50,000 = $9.60

3.018 a. 4
b. 1
c. 5
d. 2
e. 3

CONSUMER MATHEMATICS 5
SELF TEST
SOLUTION KEY

SELF TEST 1

1.01 $\frac{1}{10,000} = 10^{-4} = 10^{-1} \times 10^{-3} =$
0.1×10^{-3}
0.1 millimeter, 0.1 mm

1.02 $1,000,000 = 10^{6}$
1 megaliter, 1 Ml

1.03 $\frac{1}{1,000,000} = 10^{-6}$
1 microampere, 1 μA

1.04 $50,000 = 50 \times 10^{3}$
50 kilograms, 50 kg

1.05 $\frac{1}{1,000,000,000} = 10^{-9}$
1 nanosecond, 1 ns

1.06 Convert 15,000 feet to meters and divide by 1,000 since 1 kilometer = 1,000 meters.
$15,000 \times 3.048 \times 10^{-1} \div 1,000 =$
$15,000 \times 0.3048 \div 1,000 =$
$4,572 \div 1,000 = 4.572$ or 4.57 km

1.07 Convert 300 centimeters to feet and divide by 3 since 1 yard = 3 feet.
$300 \times \frac{1}{30.48} \div 3 =$
$\frac{300}{30.48} \div 3 =$
$\frac{100}{30.48} = 3.28$ yd.

1.08 $440 \times 9.144 \times 10^{-1} =$
$440 \times 0.9144 =$
402.336 or 402.34 m

1.09 $25\frac{1}{2} \times 2.54 =$
$25.5 \times 2.54 =$
64.77 cm

1.010 Convert 30,000 millimeters to inches and divide by 1,000 since 1 micron = 1 millionth of a meter and 1 millimeter = 1 thousandth of a meter.
$30,000 \times \frac{1}{25.4} \div 1,000 =$
$\frac{30,000}{25.4} \div 1,000 =$
$1,181.1 \div 1,000 =$
1.1811 or 1.18 in.

1.011 $40 \times 6.45 = 258$ cm^2

1.012 Convert 40,000 ft.^{2} to square meters and divide by 10,000 since 1 hectare = 10,000 square meters.
$40,000 \times 9.29 \times 10^{-2} \div 10,000 =$
$40,000 \times 0.0929 \div 10,000 =$
$3,716 \div 10,000 =$
0.3716 or 0.37 hectare

1.013 10 mm = 1 cm
100 mm^2 = 1 cm^2
500 mm^2 = 5 cm^2
$\text{cm}^2 \times \frac{1}{6.45} = \text{in.}^2$
$5 \times \frac{1}{6.45} =$
$\frac{5}{6.45} = 0.775$ in.^{2}

1.014 $10 \times 259 = 2,590$ hectares

1.015 $90 \times 8.36 \times 10^{-1} =$
$90 \times 0.836 =$
75.24 m^2

1.016 **1 ft^3. = 2.832×10^{-2} m^3**

$10 \times 2.832 \times 10^{-2} = 28.32 \times 10^{-2}$ m^3
= .283 m^3
= 2.83×10^{-1} m^3

1.017 **1 qt = 946.36 cm^3**

$\frac{1500}{946.36} = 1.59$ qts

1.018 $17 \times 3.785 = 64.345$ l

1.019 $3.5 \times \frac{1}{3.785} =$

$\frac{3.5}{3.785} =$

0.925 gal.

1.020 $50 \times 9.463 \times 10^{-1} =$

$50 \times 0.9463 =$

47.315 or 47.32 l

1.021 $6{,}000 \times \frac{1}{453.59} =$

$\frac{6{,}000}{453.59} =$

13.23 lb.

1.022 Convert 450 grains to milligrams and divide by 1,000 since 1 gram = 1,000 milligrams.

$450 \times 64.798 \div 1{,}000 =$

$29{,}159.1 \div 1{,}000 =$

29.1591 or 29.16 gm

1.023 $85 \times \frac{1}{4.536 \times 10^{-1}} =$

$85 \times \frac{1}{0.4536} =$

$\frac{85}{0.4536} =$

187.39 lb.

1.024 $\frac{3}{4} \times 9.072 \times 10^{-1} =$

$0.75 \times 0.9072 =$

0.6804 or 0.68 metric ton

1.025 $6{,}000 \times \frac{1}{907.2} = \frac{6{,}000}{907.2} =$

6.61 tons

1.026 c

$°C = (98.6 - 32) \times \frac{5}{9}$

$= 66.6 \times \frac{5}{9}$

$= \frac{333}{9}$

= 37 C

1.027 d

$°C = (69.98 - 32) \times \frac{5}{9}$

$= 37.98 \times \frac{5}{9}$

$= \frac{189.9}{9}$

= 21.1°C

1.028 b

$°C = (5{,}072 - 32) \times \frac{5}{9}$

$= 5{,}040 \times \frac{5}{9}$

= 2,800°C

1.029 a

$°C = (3{,}000 - 32) \times \frac{5}{9}$

$= 2{,}968 \times \frac{5}{9}$

$= \frac{14{,}840}{9}$

= 1,649°C

1.030 e

$°C = (110 - 32) \times \frac{5}{9}$

$= 78 \times \frac{5}{9}$

$= \frac{390}{9}$

= 43.3°C

SELF TEST 2

2.01 $10.5 \times 2.54 = 26.67$ cm

$A = \frac{1}{2}bh$

$A = \frac{1}{2}(15)(26.67)$

$A = 200.025$ or 200 cm^2

2.02 $A = \frac{1}{2}bh$

$100 = \frac{1}{2}(20)h$

$100 = 10h$

$\frac{100}{10} = h$

$h = 10$ cm

2.03

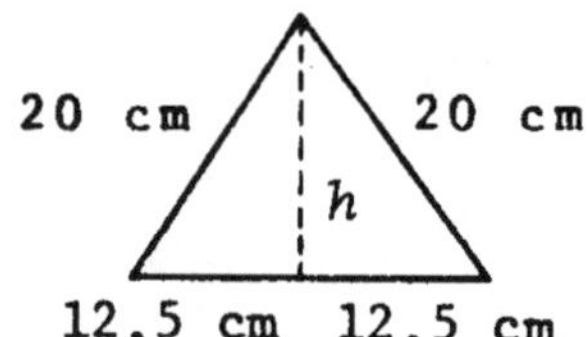

2.03 cont.

$12.5^2 + h^2 = 20^2$
$h^2 = 20^2 - 12.5^2$
$h^2 = 400 - 156.25$
$h^2 = 243.75$
$\sqrt{h^2} = \sqrt{243.75}$
$h = 15.613$ cm

$A = \frac{1}{2}bh$
$A = \frac{1}{2}(25)(15.613)$
$A = 195.16$ cm^2

2.04 $A = 15 \times 19.5$
$A = 292.5$ ft.^{2}
$A = 292.5 \times 9.29 \times 10^{-2}$
$A = 292.5 \times 0.0929$
$A = 27.17325$ or 27.17 m^2

2.05 $A = \frac{1}{2}(a + b)h$
$A = \frac{1}{2}(25 + 35)(10)$
$A = \frac{1}{2}(60)(10)$
$A = 300$ cm^2

2.06 $A = 4 \times 4$
$A = 16$ ft.^{2}
$A = 16 \times 9.29 \times 10^{-2}$
$A = 16 \times 0.0929$
$A = 1.4864$ or 1.49 m^2

2.07 $A = \pi r^2$
$A = 3.14(8)^2$
$A = 3.14(64)$
$A = 200.96$ or 201 cm^2

2.08 $C = 2\pi r$
$28 = 2(3.14)r$
$28 = 6.28r$
$\frac{28}{6.28} = r$
$r = 4.458598$ or 4.46 cm

2.09 $A = \pi ab$
$a = \frac{1}{2}(10) = 5$ cm
$b = \frac{1}{2}(14) = 7$ cm
$A = 3.14(5)(7)$
$A = 109.9$ or 110 cm^2

2.010 $C = 2\pi r$
$100 = 2(3.14)r$
$100 = 6.28r$
$\frac{100}{6.28} = r$
$r = 15.924$ cm

2.010 cont.

$A = \pi r^2$
$A = 3.14(15.924)^2$
$A = 3.14(253.57)$
$A = 796.21$ cm^2

2.011 Let the ratio be $3x:2x$.
$2a = 3x$; $a = \frac{1}{2}(3x) = \frac{3}{2}x$ or $1.5x$
$2b = 2x$; $b = \frac{1}{2}(2x) = x$

$A = \pi ab$
$150 = 3.14(1.5x)(x)$
$150 = 3.14(1.5x^2)$
$150 = 4.71x^2$
$\frac{150}{4.71} = x^2$
$x^2 = 31.847$
$\sqrt{x^2} = \sqrt{31.847}$
$x = 5.64$ cm
$1.5x = 1.5(5.64) = 8.46$ cm

Major semiaxis = 8.46 cm;
minor semiaxis = 5.64 cm.

2.012 A(square) = $10 \times 10 = 100$ in.^{2}
A(circle) = $\pi r^2 = 3.14(5)^2 = 3.14(25) = 78.5$ in.^{2}

$A = 100 - 78.5$
$= 21.5$ in.^{2}

2.013

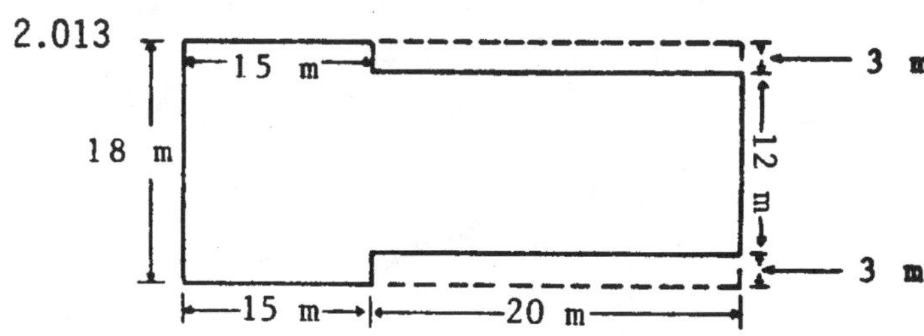

A (parking area) = 18 m × 15 m
= 270 m^2
A (driveway) = 20 m × 12 m
= 240 m^2
Total area = 270 + 240
= 510 m^2

2.014 A (larger circle) $= \pi r^2 = 3.14(7)^2$
$= 3.14(49)$
$= 153.86$ in.^{2}
A (smaller circle) $= \pi r^2$
$= 3.14(4)^2$
$= 3.14(16)$
$= 50.24$ in.^{2}
A (exposed area of brass ring) $= 153.86 - 50.24$
$= 103.62$ in.^{2}

2.015 A (floors) $= 6 \times 75 \times 40$
$= 18{,}000$ m^2
A (stairwell) $= 6 \times 2.5 \times 1.5$
$= 22.5$ m^2
A (floor to be carpeted) $= 18{,}000 - 22.5$
$= 17{,}977.5$ m^2

2.016 A (2 trapezoids) $= 2 \times \frac{1}{2}(2.6 + 1.8)(1)$
$= 2 \times \frac{1}{2}(4.4)(1)$
$= 2 \times 2.2$
$= 4.4$ m^2
A (2 trapezoids) $= 2 \times \frac{1}{2}(2.2 + 1.5)(1)$
$= 2 \times \frac{1}{2}(3.7)(1)$
$= 2 \times 1.85$
$= 3.7$ m^2
A (bottom) $= 1.8 \times 1.5 = 2.7$ m^2
Total area $= 4.4 + 3.7 + 2.7$
$= 10.8$ m^2

2.017

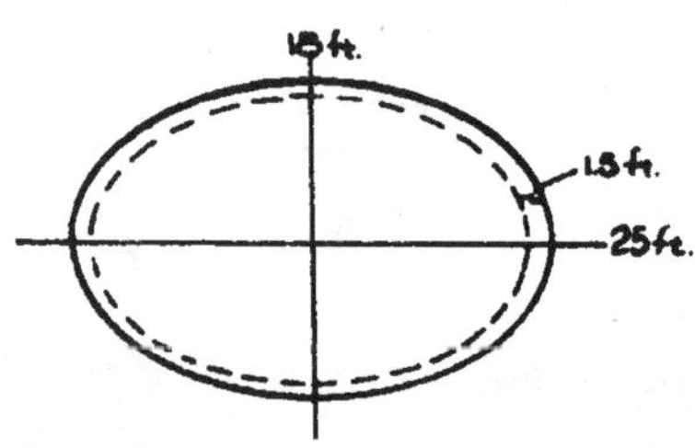

Length of minor semiaxis $= \frac{1}{2}(18) + 1.5$
$= 9 + 1.5$
$= 10.5$ ft.
Length of major semiaxis $= \frac{1}{2}(25) + 1.5$
$= 12.5 + 1.5$
$= 14$ ft.

2.017 cont.

$A = \pi ab$
$A = 3.14(14)(10.5)$
$A = 461.58$ ft.^{2}

2.018 A (storage shed) $= 4 \times 5 \times 8$
$= 160$ ft.^{2}
Number of gallons needed $= \frac{160}{160} = 1$ gallon

SELF TEST 3

3.01 $\frac{1}{1{,}000} = 10^{-3}$
1 milliliter, 1 ml

3.02 $1{,}000{,}000 = 10^6$
1 megaton, 1 Mt

3.03 $10{,}000 = 10^4 = 10 \times 10^3$
10 kilocycles, 10 kc

3.04 $500 \times 3.048 \times 10^{-1} =$
$500 \times 0.3048 =$
152.4 m

3.05 $120 \times \frac{1}{9.144 \times 10^{-1}} =$
$120 \times \frac{1}{0.9144} =$
$\frac{120}{0.9144} =$
131.23 yd.

3.06 $1{,}000 \times \frac{1}{30.48} =$
$\frac{1{,}000}{30.48} =$
32.81 ft.

3.07 $25 \times 6.45 = 161.25$ cm^2

3.08 $1{,}000 \times \frac{1}{8.36 \times 10^{-1}} =$
$1{,}000 \times \frac{1}{0.836} =$
$\frac{1{,}000}{0.836} =$
1,196.17 yd.^{2}

3.09 $250 \times \frac{1}{4.05 \times 10^{-1}} =$

$250 \times \frac{1}{0.405} =$

$\frac{250}{0.405} =$

617.28 acres

3.010 $50 \times \frac{1}{1.164 \times 4.732 \times 10^{-1}} =$

$50 \times \frac{1}{1.164 \times 0.4732} =$

$50 \times \frac{1}{0.5508} =$

$\frac{50}{0.5508} =$

90.78 pt.(dry)

3.011 $3 \times 946.36 = 2{,}839.08 \text{ cm}^3$

3.012 $100 \times \frac{1}{29.574} =$

$\frac{100}{29.574} = 3.38$ fluid oz.

3.013 $200 \times 4.536 \times 10^{-1} =$

$200 \times 0.4536 =$

90.72 kg

3.014 $1{,}000 \times \frac{1}{28.35} =$

$\frac{1{,}000}{28.35} =$

35.27 oz.

3.015 $°F = \frac{9}{5} \times 1{,}500 + 32$

$= 2{,}700 + 32$

$= 2{,}732°F$

3.016 $A = \frac{1}{2}bh$

$A = \frac{1}{2}(6)(4)$

$A = 12 \text{ m}^2$

3.017 $A = \frac{1}{2}(a + b)h$

$A = \frac{1}{2}(8.5 + 4.5)(6.5)$

$A = \frac{1}{2}(13)(6.5)$

$A = 42.25 \text{ m}^2$

3.018 $A = \pi ab$

$A = 3.14(20)(14)$

$A = 879.2 \text{ cm}^2$

3.019 10' 6" x 12' 3" =

10.5' x 12.25' =

128.625 ft.^2

3.020 A (2 walls) $= 2 \times 18 \times 8$

$= 288 \text{ ft.}^2$

A (2 walls) $= 2 \times 9 \times 8$

$= 144 \text{ ft.}^2$

Total area (walls) $= 288 + 144$

$= 432 \text{ ft.}^2$

A (each panel) $= 4 \times 8$

$= 32 \text{ ft.}^2$

Number of panels needed $= \frac{432}{32} = 13.5$

$= 14$ panels

3.021 $A = 6a^2$

$A = 6(5.5)^2$

$A = 6(30.25)$

$A = 181.5 \text{ cm}^2$

3.022 $V = \frac{1}{3}(3.5 \times 3.5)(4.7)$

$V = \frac{1}{3}(12.25)(4.7)$

$V = 19.191667 \text{ in.}^3$

$V = \frac{19.191667}{1{,}728} \text{ ft.}^3$

$V = 0.0111063 \text{ ft.}^3$

$V = 0.0111063 \times 2.832 \times 10^{-2}$

$V = 0.0111063 \times 0.02832$

$V = 0.0003145 \text{ m}^3$

$V = 314.5 \text{ cm}^3$

3.023 $V = 10 \times 6.5 \times 8.3$

$= 539.5 \text{ cm}^3$

3.024 $V = a^3$

$V = (3.2)^3$

$V = 32.768$ or 32.77 cm^3

3.025 $A = 2(4 \times 5 + 4 \times 10 + 5 \times 10)$

$A = 2(20 + 40 + 50)$

$A = 2(110)$

$A = 220 \text{ in.}^2$

3.026 $A = \frac{1}{2}(8.4)(5.5)$

$A = 23.1 \text{ m}^2$

3.027 $V = \pi abh$

$V = 3.14(6)(4)(7.5)$

$V = 565.2 \text{ cm}^3$

3.028 $A = 4\pi r^2$
$A = 4(3.14)(4)^2$
$A = 4(3.14)(16)$
$A = 200.96 \text{ in.}^2$
$A = 200.96 \times 6.45$
$A = 1296.192$ or 1296.19 cm^2

3.029 $A = \pi r\sqrt{r^2 + h^2}$
$A = 3.14(3.5)\sqrt{3.5^2 + 14^2}$
$A = 3.14(3.5)\sqrt{12.25 + 196}$
$A = 3.14(3.5)\sqrt{208.25}$
$A = 10.99\sqrt{208.25}$
$A = 10.99(14.43)$
$A = 158.59 \text{ cm}^2$

3.030 $V = \frac{1}{3}\pi r^2 h$
$V = \frac{1}{3}(3.14)(5)^2(10)$
$V = \frac{1}{3}(3.14)(25)(10)$
$V = 261.6666 \text{ in.}^3$
$V = \frac{261.6666}{1,728} \text{ ft.}^3$
$V = 0.1514274$
$V = 0.1514274 \times 2.832 \times 10^{-2}$
$V = 0.1514274 \times 0.02832$
$V = 0.0042884 \text{ m}^3$
$V = 4,288.4 \text{ cm}^3$

3.031 $V = \frac{4}{3}\pi r^3$
$V = \frac{4}{3}(3.14)(3)^3$
$V = \frac{4}{3}(3.14)(27)$
$V = 113.04 \text{ in.}^3$

3.032 $V = \pi r^2 h$
$r = \frac{1}{2}(10) = 5 \text{ cm}$
$V = 3.14(5)^2(20)$
$V = 3.14(25)(20)$
$V = 1,570 \text{ cm}^3$

3.033 $V = \pi r^2 h$
$r = \frac{1}{2}(8.5) = 4.25 \text{ in.}$
$= 4.25 \times 2.54 = 10.795 \text{ cm}$
$h = 10 \text{ in.} = 10 \times 2.54 = 25.4 \text{ cm}$
$V = 3.14(10.795)^2(25.4)$
$V = 3.14(116.53203)(25.4)$
$V = 9,294.1285 \text{ cm}^3$
$V = 9.294$ liters

3.034 0.5 m = 50 cm
3 m = 300 cm
V (solid wall) $= 25 \times 50 \times 300$
$= 375,000 \text{ cm}^3$
V (cut out portion) $= 25 \times 60 \times 10$
$= 15,000 \text{ cm}^3$
V (wall) $= 375,000 - 15,000$
$= 360,000 \text{ cm}^3$
V (each cement block) $= 10 \times 4 \times 2$
$= 80 \text{ cm}^3$

Number of cement blocks needed $= \frac{360,000}{80} = 4,500$ blocks

3.035 $A = 2\pi rh = \pi dh$
$225 = 3.14(d)9.5)$
$225 = 29.83d$
$\frac{225}{29.83} = d$
$d = 7.54 \text{ cm}$

3.036 V (each piling) $= 20 \times 2 \times 2$
$= 80 \text{ ft.}^3$
V (10 pilings) $= 10 \times 80$
$= 800 \text{ ft.}^3$

3.037 $A = \frac{1}{2}(16)(8)$
$A = 64 \text{ ft.}^2$

CONSUMER MATHEMATICS 6
SELF TEST
SOLUTION KEY

SELF TEST 1

1.01
$$\begin{array}{r} \$20.00 \\ -\ 19.43 \\ \hline \$\ 0.57 \end{array}$$

1.02
$$\begin{array}{r} \$100.00 \\ -\ 62.48 \\ \hline \$\ 37.52 \end{array}$$

1.03
$$\begin{array}{r} \$60.00 \\ -\ 42.28 \\ \hline \$17.72 \end{array}$$

1.04 4% + 7% = 11%
$38.50 x 0.11 = 4.235 = $4.24

1.05 $5.50 x 0.06 = $0.33 tax
$5.50 + 0.33 = $5.83

1.06
$$\$7.02 = 0.08(\text{price}) + \text{price}$$
$$\$7.02 = \text{price}(0.08 + 1)$$
$$\$7.02 = \text{price}(1.08)$$
$$\frac{\$7.02}{1.08} = \text{price}$$
$$\text{price} = \$6.50$$

1.07
$$\frac{\$460}{\$6{,}595} = 0.0697 = 7\%$$

1.08 Total payments made for 5 years (60 months) = 60 x $258.50 = $15,510.
Total amount of interest = $15,510 - 10,000 = $5,510.

$y = 12$
$c = \$5{,}510$
$m = \$10{,}000$
$n = 60$

$$I = \frac{2(12 \times 5{,}510)}{10{,}000(60 + 1)}$$
$$= \frac{2(66{,}120)}{10{,}000(61)}$$
$$= \frac{132{,}240}{610{,}000}$$
$$= 0.217$$
$$= 21.7\%$$

1.09 $I = 18\% = 0.18$
$y = 12$
$m = \$495 - 50 = \$445$
$n = 36$

Find c:
$$0.18 = \frac{2(12 \times c)}{445(36 + 1)}$$
$$0.18 = \frac{2(12c)}{445(37)}$$
$$0.18 = \frac{24c}{16{,}465}$$
$$\frac{0.18(16{,}465)}{24} = c$$
$$\frac{2{,}963.7}{24} = c$$
$$c = 123.4875$$
$$= \$123.49$$
$$\text{Monthly payments} = \frac{445 + 123.49}{36}$$
$$= \frac{568.49}{36}$$
$$= \$15.79$$

1.010 $I = 12\% = 0.12$
$y = 12$
$m = \$15{,}000 - 2{,}250$
$= \$12{,}750$
$n = 5 \text{ years} = 60 \text{ months}$

Find c:
$$0.12 = \frac{2(12 \times c)}{12{,}750(60 + 1)}$$
$$0.12 = \frac{2(12c)}{12{,}750(61)}$$
$$0.12 = \frac{24c}{777{,}750}$$
$$\frac{0.12(777{,}750)}{24} = c$$
$$\frac{93{,}330}{24} = c$$
$$c = \$3{,}888.75$$
$$\text{Monthly payments} = \frac{12{,}750 + 3{,}888.75}{60}$$
$$= \frac{16{,}638.75}{60}$$
$$= 277.3125$$
$$= \$277.31$$

1.011
$$\$225 = (\$195 \times \text{markup}) + \$195$$
$$\$225 - \$195 = \$195 \times \text{markup}$$
$$\frac{\$30}{\$195} = \text{markup} = .154 = 15\%$$

1.012 $\$2,150(1 - 0.18) = \$2,150(0.82) = \$1,763$

1.013 price = ($455 x .28) + $455

= $127.40 + $455

= $582.40

1.014 Let x = cost

$\$555 = .35x + x$

$\$555 = 1.35x$

$\frac{\$555}{1.35} = x = \$411.11$

1.015 $1,895 = ($1,755 x markup) + $1,755

$1,895 - $1,755 = $1,755 x markup

$\frac{\$140}{\$1755} = \text{markup}$

markup = .0798 = 8%

1.016 $\$135 - 115 = \$20$

$\frac{\$20}{\$135} = 0.148 = 14.8\%$

1.017 $9.98 = 0.04(price) + price
$9.98 = price(0.04 + 1)
$9.98 = price(1.04)

$\frac{\$9.98}{1.04} = \text{price}$

price = $9.60

$9.60 = ($8.75 x markup) + $8.75

$9.60 - $8.75 = $8.75 x markup

$\frac{\$0.85}{\$8.75} = \text{markup} = 0.097 = 10\%$

SELF TEST 2

2.01 Sales Workers

2.02 Male: $\frac{207,000 - 9,000}{9,000} = \frac{198,000}{9,000} = 22 = 2,200\%$

Female: $\frac{51,000 - 4,000}{4,000} = \frac{47,000}{4,000} = 11.75 = 1,175\%$

2.03 Self-employed Managers

2.04 Males: Bank Tellers
Females: Sales Workers

2.05 $\frac{\$4,190 - \$3,860}{\$3,860} = \frac{\$330}{\$3,860} = 0.085 = 8.5\%$

2.06 1939

2.07 1945

2.08 1939-1944

2.09 From 20% to 75% or a range of 55%

2.010 down (the percentage of business failures rose)

2.011 $\$7,500 - 4,500 = \$3,000$

2.012 $\frac{\$7,500 - \$4,500}{\$4,500} = \frac{\$3,000}{\$4,500} = 0.67 = 67\%$

2.013 $\frac{\$11,800 - \$8,060}{\$8,060} = \frac{\$3,740}{\$8,060} = 0.464 = 46.4\%$

2.014 yes

2.015 Males: $11,800
Females: $6,600
Difference = $\$11,800 - 6,600 = \$5,200$

2.016 $\frac{50 \text{ minutes}}{85 \text{ customers}} = \frac{? \text{ minutes}}{200 \text{ customers}}$

$\frac{50(200)}{85}$ = no. of minutes

$\frac{10,000}{85}$ = no. of minutes

no. of minutes = 117.6

117.6 minutes = about 2 hours

2.017 Eating area = 60 x 50
= 3,000 ft.^{2}

3,000 x 20% =
3,000 x 0.2 = 600 ft.^{2}
Total area = 3,000 + 600
= 3,600 ft.^{2}

2.018 Area of garage = 250 x 180
= 45,000 ft.^{2}

Space available for servicing = $\frac{45,000}{2}$
= 22,500 ft.^{2}

Number of vehicles = $\frac{22,500}{250}$
= 90

2.019 Area of garage = 165 x 130
= 21,450 ft.^{2}

Space available for servicing = $\frac{21,450}{2}$
= 10,725 ft.^{2}

Number of vehicles = $\frac{10,725}{250}$
= 42.9
= 43

Since you can service only 43 vehicles at a time and you need to be able to service 65 vehicles at a time, the projected amount of space will not be adequate.

2.020 150 x \$2.95 x 20% =
150 x \$2.95 x 0.2 = \$88.50

2.021 price = (\$3,050 x .15) + \$3,050
= \$457.50 + \$3,050
= \$3,507.50

2.022 \$275 x 100% =
\$275 x 1.00 = \$275 markup

\$275 + \$275 = \$550 retail price

\$550(1 - 0.25) =
\$550(0.75) = \$412.50

2.023 \$5.75(1 - 0.1) =
\$5.75(0.9) = \$5.18 discounted price

\$5.18 x 0.04 = \$0.21 tax

Total price = \$5.18 + 0.21
= \$5.39

2.024 \$10.00
\- 5.39
\$ 4.61

2.025 $I = \frac{2(yc)}{m(n + 1)}$

I = 18% = 0.18
y = 12
m = \$48
n = 12

Find c:

$0.18 = \frac{2(12 \times c)}{48(12 + 1)}$

$0.18 = \frac{2(12c)}{48(13)}$

$0.18 = \frac{24c}{624}$

$\frac{0.18(624)}{24} = c$

$\frac{112.32}{24} = c$

c = \$4.68

Monthly payments = $\frac{48 + 4.68}{12}$
= $\frac{52.68}{12}$
= \$4.39

2.026 $I = \frac{2(yc)}{m(n + 1)}$

$y = 12$
$c = \$1,500 - 1,000$
$= \$500$
$m = \$1,000$
$n = 2$ years $= 24$ months

$I = \frac{2(12 \times 500)}{1,000(24 + 1)}$
$= \frac{2(6,000)}{1,000(25)}$
$= \frac{12,000}{25,000}$
$= 0.48$
$= 48\%$

2.027 $15 + 3.50 = $18.50 before tax
$18.95 - 18.50 = $0.45 tax
$\frac{\$0.45}{\$3.50} = 0.129 = 12.9\%$

SELF TEST 3

3.01 $R = \frac{E}{I} = \frac{12}{60} = 0.2$ ohm

3.02 $E = RI = 0.11(55) = 6.05$ or 6 volts

3.03 $\frac{35}{70} = \frac{\text{speed of countershaft drive gear}}{450}$

speed of countershaft drive gear $= \frac{35(450)}{70}$
$= \frac{450}{2}$
$= 225$ r.p.m.

3.04 $3,000 \div 3 = 1,000$ r.p.m.

3.05 $825 \times 1\frac{2}{3} =$
$825 \times \frac{5}{3} = 1,375$ r.p.m.

3.06 $\text{weight}_1 \times \text{distance}_1 =$
$\text{weight}_2 \times \text{distance}_2$

3.06 $750 \times d_1 = 150 \times d_2$
$750 \times d_1 = 150 \times (15 - d_1)$
$750d_1 = 2,250 - 150d_1$
$750d_1 + 150d_1 = 2,250$
$900d_1 = 2,250$
$\frac{900d_1}{900} = \frac{2,250}{900}$
$d_1 = 2.5'$
$d_2 = 15 - 2.5 = 12.5'$

3.07 $\frac{d_a}{d_b} = \frac{\text{r.p.m.}_b}{\text{r.p.m.}_a}$

$\frac{1.5}{3} = \frac{\text{r.p.m.}_b}{300}$
$\frac{1.5(300)}{3} = \text{r.p.m.}_b$
$\frac{450}{3} = \text{r.p.m.}_b$
$\text{r.p.m.}_b = 150$ r.p.m.

Since pulleys B and C are keyed together, $\text{r.p.m.}_b = \text{r.p.m.}_c = 150$ r.p.m.

$\frac{d_c}{d_d} = \frac{\text{r.p.m.}_d}{\text{r.p.m.}_c}$
$\frac{1}{4} = \frac{\text{r.p.m.}_d}{150}$
$\frac{1(150)}{4} = \text{r.p.m.}_d$
$\text{r.p.m.}_d = 37.5$ r.p.m.

3.08 $\frac{d_d}{d_c} = \frac{\text{r.p.m.}_c}{\text{r.p.m.}_d}$

$\frac{7}{2} = \frac{\text{r.p.m.}_c}{100}$
$\frac{7(100)}{2} = \text{r.p.m.}_c$
$\frac{700}{2} = \text{r.p.m.}_c$
$\text{r.p.m.}_c = 350$ r.p.m.

3.08 cont.

Since pulleys B and C are keyed together,
$r.p.m._b = r.p.m._c = 350$ r.p.m.

$$\frac{d_b}{d_a} = \frac{r.p.m._a}{r.p.m._b}$$
$$\frac{5.25}{3.5} = \frac{r.p.m._a}{350}$$
$$\frac{5.25(350)}{3.5} = r.p.m._a$$
$$\frac{1,837.5}{3.5} = r.p.m._a$$
$$r.p.m._a = 525 \text{ r.p.m.}$$

3.09 $F \times d_h = W \times d_a$
$F \times 35 = 875 \times 4$
$35F = 3,500$
$\frac{35F}{35} = \frac{3,500}{35}$
$F = 100$ lb.

3.010 No. of oz. needed = 275 x 7
= 1,925 oz.

No. of cans needed = $\frac{1,925}{115}$
= 16.7 or 17 cans

3.011 66(2.5) = 165 servings

3.012 Calories used = weight x calorie-use factor

84 = 126 x calorie-use factor

calorie-use factor = $\frac{84}{126} = \frac{2}{3}$

Since the $\frac{2}{3}$ calorie-use factor is associated with the 6-minute mile, she must run the mile in 6 minutes.

3.013 Labor cost = \$12.00 x $3\frac{1}{2}$
= \$42.00
Overhead cost = \$42.00 x $0.66\frac{2}{3}$
= \$28.00
Cost of parts = \$112.50
Total cost = \$42.00 + 28.00 + 112.50
= \$182.50

3.014 \$147.51 - 32.50 = \$115.01

Let x = labor cost.

labor cost + overhead cost = \$115.01

$x + 0.55x = \$115.01$
$1x + 0.55x = \$115.01$
$1.55x = \$115.01$
$\frac{1.55x}{1.55} = \frac{\$115.01}{1.55}$
$x = \$74.20$

Hourly rate = \$74.20 ÷ 5
= \$14.84

3.015 Labor charge = \$14 x 40
= \$560
Overhead charge = \$560 x 1.25
= \$700
Price of goods = \$85 + 85(0.06)
= \$85 + 5.10
= \$90.10
Total bill = \$560 + 700 + 90.10
= \$1,350.10

3.016 $\frac{1,400}{20}$ = 70 people

3.017 Area of garage = 300 x 165
= 49,500 ft.^{2}
Space available for servicing = $\frac{49,500}{2}$
= 24,750 ft.^{2}
Number of automobiles = 2 x $\frac{24,750}{250}$
= 2 x 99
= 198 automobiles

3.018 The cafeteria line is open 90 minutes. The first customer takes 8 minutes to proceed through the line and pay the cashier. The remaining customers proceed through the line at the rate of 1 customer every 30 seconds (or 1 customer every $\frac{1}{2}$ minute) during the remaining 82 minutes. No customers follow the last customer, and the last customer pays as the line is closed.

8 minutes	-	first customer
82 minutes	-	164 customers
90 minutes	-	165 customers

3.019 Station space = 8 x 36
= 288 ft.^{2}
Total present space = 288 + 216
= 504 ft.^{2}
Additional station space = 2 x 36
= 72 ft.^{2}
Proportion of new additional space needed = $\frac{2}{8}$ = $\frac{1}{4}$.
New additional space = $\frac{1}{4}$ x 216
= 54 ft.^{2}
Total area = 504 + 72 + 54
= 630 ft.^{2}

3.020 4-6 years and 6-8 years, or 4-8 years

3.021

0-2 years:	100,000
2-4 years:	200,000
4-6 years:	300,000
6-8 years:	300,000
More than 8:	100,000
Total:	1,000,000

3.022 2-4 years: 200,000
Total: 1,000,000

$\frac{200,000}{1,000,000} = 0.2 = 20\%$

3.023 \$48.50(1 - 0.125) =
\$48.50(0.875) = \$42.44 discounted price
\$42.44(11%) =
\$42.44(0.11) = \$4.67 tax
\$42.44 + 4.67 = \$47.11

3.024 \$110 x 0.06 = \$6.60

3.025 \$15.00 - 14.27 = \$0.73

3.026 price = (\$31.55 x 0.17) + \$31.55
= \$5.36 + \$31.55
= \$36.91

3.027 \$8.50(1 - 0.15) =
\$8.50(0.85) = \$7.23 discounted price
\$7.23(0.05) = \$0.36 tax
\$7.23 + 0.36 = \$7.59

3.028 \$6.50 x 6 = \$39.00

$\frac{\$39.00 - 32.50}{\$39.00} = \frac{\$6.50}{\$39.00}$
$= 0.16\frac{2}{3}$
$= 16\frac{2}{3}\%$

3.029 Total payments made for 36 months = 36 x \$79.50 = \$2,862.

Total amount of interest = \$2,862 - 2,500 = \$362.

y = 12
c = \$362
m = \$2,500
n = 36

$$I = \frac{2(12 \times 362)}{2,500(36 + 1)}$$
$$= \frac{2(4,344)}{2,500(37)}$$
$$= \frac{8,688}{92,500}$$
$$= 0.094$$
$$= 9.4\%$$

3.030 Total payments made for 20 months = \$16.50 x 20 = \$330.00.

Principal = \$315.50 - 31.55 = \$283.95.

3.030 cont.

Total amount of interest =
$330.00 - 283.95 = $46.05.

y = 12
c = $46.05
m = $283.95
n = 20

$$I = \frac{2(12 \times 46.05)}{283.95(20 + 1)}$$
$$= \frac{2(552.6)}{283.95(21)}$$
$$= \frac{1,105.2}{5,962.95}$$
$$= 0.185$$
$$= 18.5\%$$

CONSUMER MATHEMATICS 7
SELF TEST
SOLUTION KEY

SELF TEST 1

1.01
$c = \$205 \times 48 - \$6,785$
$= \$9,840 - \$6,785$
$= \$3,055$
$I = \frac{2(12)(3,055)}{6,785(48 + 1)}$
$= \frac{2(12)(3,055)}{6,785(49)}$
$= \frac{73,320}{332,465}$
$= 0.22$
$= 22\%$

1.02
$c = \$165 \times 28 - (\$4,500 - \$450)$
$= \$165 \times 28 - \$4,050$
$= \$4,620 - \$4,050$
$= \$570$
$I = \frac{2(12)(570)}{4,050(28 + 1)}$
$= \frac{2(12)(570)}{4,050(29)}$
$= \frac{13,680}{117,450}$
$= 0.116$
$= 11.6\%$

1.03
$c = 168 \times n - (\$6,800 - \$700)$
$= 168 \times n - \$6,100$
$0.158 = \frac{2(12)(168 \times n - 6,100)}{6,100(n + 1)}$
$0.158 = \frac{24(168n - 6,100)}{6,100(n + 1)}$
$0.158(6,100) \cdot (n + 1) = 4,032n - 146,400$
$963.8(n + 1) = 4,032n - 146,400$
$963.8n + 963.8 = 4,032n - 146,400$
$963.8n + 963.8 + 146,400 = 4,032n$
$963.8n + 147,363.8 = 4,032n$
$147,363.8 = 4,032n - 963.8n$
$147,363.8 = 3,068.2n$
$\frac{147,363.8}{3,068.2} = \frac{3,068.2n}{3,068.2}$
$48 = n$

1.04
$0.192 = \frac{2(12)c}{(11,500 - 1,150)(44 + 1)}$
$0.192 = \frac{2(12)c}{10,350(45)}$
$\frac{0.192(10\ 350)(45)}{2(12)} = c$
$\frac{89,424}{24} = c$
$c = \$3,726$

Amount of monthly payment =
$\frac{\$10,350 + \$3,726}{44} =$
$\frac{\$14,076}{44} = \$319.91$

1.05 $\frac{\$1,000}{10,000} = 0.1 = 10¢$ per mile

1.06 $\frac{\$1,750}{\$0.095} = 18,421$ miles

1.07 $20,000 \times \$0.11 = \$2,200$

1.08 Total operating
cost $= \$550 + \$125 + \$120$
$= \$795$
cost $= \frac{\$795}{14,000}$
$= 0.057$
$= 5.7¢$ per mile

1.09 Total operating
cost $= \$150 + \$85 + \$125$
$= \$360$
Miles driven $= \frac{\$360}{\$0.045}$
$= 8,000$ miles

1.010 Total operating
cost $= \$1,950 + \$1,200 + \$900 + \$240$
$= \$4,290$
Operating cost $= \frac{\$4,290}{17,000}$
$= 0.252$
$= 25.2¢$ per mile

1.011 Total operating
cost $= \$1,200 + \$1,000 + \$850 + \$250$
$= \$3,300$

1.011 cont.

$$\text{Operating cost} = \frac{\$3,300}{18,000} = 0.183 = 18.3¢ \text{ per mile}$$

1.012 Total depreciation = $4,500 - $1,850 = $2,650

$$\text{Average yearly depreciation} = \frac{\$2,650}{6} = \$441.67$$

$$\text{Cost of depreciation} = \frac{\$441.67}{15,000} = 0.029 = 2.9¢ \text{ per mile}$$

1.013 Total depreciation = $5,700 - $3,700 = $2,000

$$\text{Average yearly depreciation} = \frac{\$2,000}{4} = \$500$$

$$\text{Average miles driven per year} = \frac{\$500}{\$0.04} = 12,500 \text{ miles}$$

1.014 Total depreciation = $6,100 - $200 = $5,900

$$\text{Average yearly depreciation} = \frac{\$5,900}{10} = \$590$$

$$\text{Cost of depreciation} = \frac{\$590}{16,000} = 0.037 = 3.7¢ \text{ per mile}$$

1.015 Average yearly depreciation = 14,125 x $0.03 = $423.75

Total depreciation = $423.75 x 4 = $1,695

Resale value = $3;995 - $1,695 = $2,300

1.016 $$\frac{\$365 - \$250}{\$250} = \frac{\$115}{\$250} = 0.46 = 46\%$$

1.017 $$\frac{\$45 - \$35}{\$35} = \frac{\$10}{\$35} = 0.286 = 28.6\%$$

1.018 Policy *A* premium = $135.00 + $75.00 + $68.00 + $17.50 + $7.00 = $302.50

Policy *B* premium = $145.00 + $71.00 + $62.00 + $14.50 + $8.40 = $300.90

Policy *B* is less expensive.

1.019 $302.50 - $300.90 = $1.60

SELF TEST 2

2.01 c = $198 x 48 - ($8,500 - $850) = $9,504 - $7,650 = $1,854

$$I = \frac{2(12)(1,854)}{7,650(48 + 1)} = \frac{2(12)(1,854)}{7,650(49)} = \frac{44,496}{374,850} = 0.119 = 11.9\%$$

2.02 Total operating cost = $780 + $125 + $240 = $1,145

$$\text{Operating cost} = \frac{\$1,145}{16,000} = 0.072 = 7.2¢ \text{ per mile}$$

2.03 Total depreciation = $3,300 - $150 = $3,150

2.03 cont.

Average yearly depreciation $= \frac{\$3,150}{10}$
$= \$315$

Cost of depreciation $= \frac{\$315}{15,000}$
$= 0.021$
= 2.1¢ per mile

2.04 Policy A premium = \$125.00 + \$85.00 + \$75.00 + \$15.50 + \$9.00
= \$309.50

Policy B premium = \$120.00 + \$82.00 + \$70.00 + \$19.50 + \$10.50
= \$302.00

Policy B appears to offer more coverage for the amount of money.

2.05 $\frac{\$309.50 - \$302.00}{\$302.00} = \frac{\$7.50}{\$302.00}$
$= 0.025$
$= 2.5\%$

2.06 Policy A = \$15.50 + \$9.00
= \$24.50

Policy B = \$19.50 + \$10.50
= \$30.00

Policy A

2.07 \$30.00 - \$24.50 = \$5.50

2.08 Policy A liability coverage = \$125.00.
Policy B liability coverage = \$120.00.
\$125.00 - \$120.00 = \$5.00 more for Policy A.
Yes, since \$5.50 is more than \$5.00.

2.09 No; if your accident rate stays the same, you will be better off to take the \$100 deductible, because you would pay more than you would get back over a 15-year span.

2.010 $d = rt = 60(2\frac{1}{4}) = 135$ miles

2.011
$$d = rt$$
$$259 = 37t$$
$$\frac{259}{37} = \frac{37t}{37}$$
$t = 7$ hours

2.012
$$d = rt$$
$$231 = r(5\tfrac{1}{2})$$
$$231 = \tfrac{11}{2}r$$
$$\frac{231}{\frac{11}{2}} = \frac{\frac{11}{2}r}{\frac{11}{2}}$$
$$r = 231(\tfrac{2}{11})$$
$= 42$ mph

2.013 First train:
$d = rt = 65(7) = 455$ miles
Second train:
$d = rt = 57(7) = 399$ miles
Distance apart = 455 + 399
= 854 miles

2.014

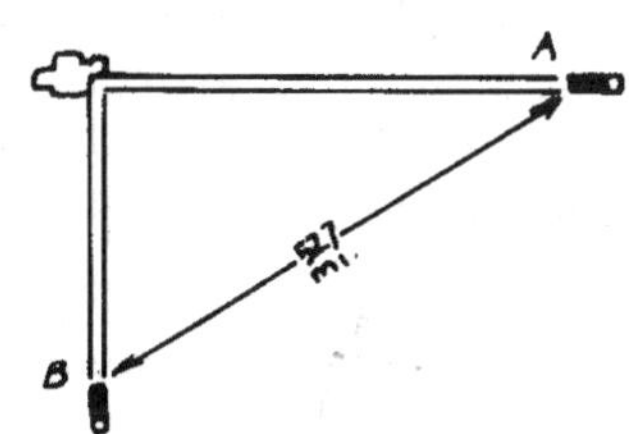

Car A:
$d = rt = 45(1) = 45$ miles
Car B:
$d = rt = 55(\frac{1}{2}) = 27.5$ miles

$(\text{distance apart})^2 = 45^2 + 27.5^2$
$= 2,025 + 756.25$
$= 2,781.25$
$\sqrt{(\text{distance apart})^2} = \sqrt{2,781.25}$
distance apart = 52.7 miles

2.015 The time difference between London and Cairo is 2 hours (5:00 p.m. to 7:00 p.m.). Add 2 hours to 8 a.m.; standard time in Cairo is 10 a.m.

2.016 Juneau is 1 hour earlier than Phoenix (9:00 a.m. to 10:00 a.m.). Subtract 1 hour from 12:00 midnight; standard time in Juneau is 11 p.m.

2.017 Honolulu is 20 hours earlier than Sydney (7:00 a.m. to 3:00 a.m. the following day). Subtract 20 hours from 6:30; Honolulu time is 10:30 p.m. the previous day.

2.018 New York is 13 hours earlier than Peking (12 noon to 1:00 a.m. the following day). Subtract 13 hours from 8 a.m.; New York time is 7 p.m. the previous night.

2.019 Normally, there is a one-hour time difference between Mountain and Pacific time zones. However, because of Daylight-Saving Time, people living in San Diego have to set their watches one hour ahead, which will make San Diego time the same as Phoenix time. Therefore, San Diego time is 6 a.m.

SELF TEST 3

3.01 $c = \$147.50 \times 24 - (\$3,500 - \$500)$
$= \$3,540 - \$3,000$
$= \$540$

$I = \frac{2(12)(540)}{3,000(24 + 1)}$
$= \frac{2(12)(540)}{3,000(25)}$
$= \frac{12,960}{75,000}$
$= 0.173$
$= 17.3\%$

3.02 Total depreciation = \$2,850 - \$1,750
= \$1,100

Average yearly depreciation = $\frac{\$1,100}{3}$
= \$366.67

Average number of miles driven = $\frac{\$366.67}{\$0.04}$
= 9,166.75 or 9,167 miles per year

3.03 $c = \$185 \times 36 - \$5,250$
$= \$6,660 - \$5,250$
$= \$1,410$

$I = \frac{2(12)(1,410)}{5,250(36 + 1)}$
$= \frac{2(12)(1,410)}{5,250(37)}$
$= \frac{33,840}{194,250}$
$= 0.174$
$= 17.4\%$

3.04 Cost of operating costs listed = \$850 + \$200
= \$1,050

Cost of servicing + \$1,050 = 18,000(\$0.09)

Cost of servicing + \$1,050 = \$1,620

Cost of servicing = \$1,620 - \$1,050
= \$570

3.05 Total depreciation = \$4,000 - \$2,500
= \$1,500

Average yearly depreciation = $\frac{\$1,500}{3}$
= \$500

3.06 Total depreciation = \$4,500 - \$3,500 = \$1,000

Total operating cost = \$1,000 + \$550 + \$275 + \$700 = \$2,525

$$\text{Operating cost} = \frac{\$2{,}525}{15{,}000} = 0.168 = 16.8¢ \text{ per mile}$$

3.07 Policy A: \$72 + \$65 = \$137
Policy B: \$75 + \$67 = \$142
Since Policy A is the most economical, Policy A is the one to buy.

3.08 $\frac{\$18 - \$14}{\$18} = \frac{\$4}{\$18} = 0.222 = 22.2\%$

3.09
$$d = rt$$
$$345 = r(7.5)$$
$$\frac{345}{7.5} = \frac{r(7.5)}{7.5}$$
$$r = 46 \text{ mph}$$

3.010 $d_{\text{Plane 1}} = d_{\text{Plane 2}}$, or
$r_{\text{Plane 1}}t_{\text{Plane 1}} = r_{\text{Plane 2}}t_{\text{Plane 2}}$

$$400(t + \tfrac{30}{60}) = 425t$$
$$400(t + \tfrac{1}{2}) = 425t$$
$$400t + 200 = 425t$$
$$200 = 425t - 400t$$
$$200 = 25t$$
$$\frac{200}{25} = \frac{25t}{25}$$
$$t = 8 \text{ hr.} + 6{:}30 \text{ p.m.} = 2{:}30 \text{ a.m.}$$

3.011

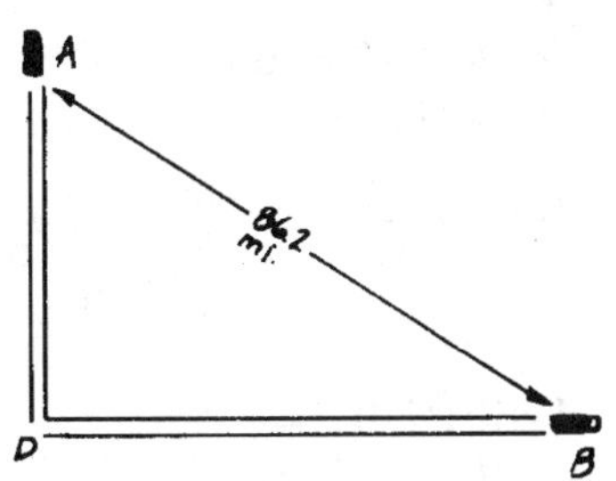

Car A:
$d = rt = 55(1\tfrac{1}{2}) = 82.5$ miles

Car B:
$d = rt = 50(\tfrac{1}{2}) = 25$ miles

$$(\text{distance apart})^2 = 82.5^2 + 25^2 = 6{,}806.25 + 625 = 7{,}431.25$$
$$\sqrt{(\text{distance apart})^2} = \sqrt{7{,}431.25}$$
$$\text{distance apart} = 86.2 \text{ miles}$$

3.012 Usually, the time difference between Phoenix and New York is 2 hours (10 a.m. to 12 noon). However, bacause of Daylight-Saving Time, residents of New York have to set their watches ahead 1 hour, making 3 hours difference between Phoenix and New York. Therefore, the time in New York is 8:00 a.m. + 3 hours, or 11:00 a.m.

3.013 London is 1 hour earlier than Warsaw (5:00 p.m. to 6:00 p.m.). Subtract 1 hour from 6:00 p.m.; standard time in London is 5:00 p.m.

3.014 15,000(.00119) = \$17.85

3.015 \$500(4.2937) = 2,146.85 bolivars

3.016 1,200(.0301) = \$36.12

3.017 11.2 + 11.6 + 12.9 + 15.8 + 16.0 + 17.4 + 39.2 + 67.5 = 191.6

$$\text{Average rate of depreciation} = \frac{191.6}{8} = 23.95\%$$

3.018 $8.1\% - 6.3\% = 1.8\%$

3.019 West Germany: 5.8
Japan: 10.2

$$\frac{10.2 - 5.8}{5.8} = \frac{4.4}{5.8} = 75.9\%$$

3.020 1950: 0.54
1976: 0.15

$$\frac{0.54 - 0.15}{0.54} = \frac{0.39}{0.54} = 0.722 = 72.2\%$$

3.021 Regular Economy Air Fare = \$440.80

14- to 21-Day Excursion Air Fare = \$331.00

$$\frac{\$440.80 - \$331.00}{\$440.80} = \frac{\$109.8}{\$440.80} = 0.249 = \text{approx. } 25\%$$

3.022 \$20.80 - \$14.37 = \$6.43

3.023 \$22.53 - \$14.69 = \$7.84 daily

3.024 Duty levied on chinaware = \$125(0.35) = \$43.75

Duty levied on 18-jewel watch = \$10.75

Difference = \$43.75 - \$10.75 = \$33.00

3.025 \$15,000 - \$100 = \$14,900
\$14,900($6\frac{1}{2}\%$) =
\$14,900(0.065) =
\$968.50

3.026 372 - 360 = 12 mph

3.027 74 - 51 = 23 more

CONSUMER MATHEMATICS 8
SELF TEST
SOLUTION KEY

SELF TEST 1

1.01 false

1.02 true

1.03 false

1.04 true

1.05 true

1.06

Assets		Liabilities	
Cash	$ 5,000($4,500 + $500)	Accounts Payable	$ 4,200
Accounts Receivable	500($0 + $500)	Owner's Equity	
Equipment	7,000	Investment	8,300($7,300 + $1,000)
Total Assets	$12,500	Total Liabilities and Owner's Equity	$12,500

1.07

Assets		Liabilities	
Cash	$ 5,000	Accounts Payable	$ 6,600($4,200 + $2,400)
Accounts Receivable	500	Owner's Equity	
Equipment	9,400($7,000 + $2,400)	Investment	8,300
Total Assets	$14,900	Total Liabilities and Owner's Equity	$14,900

1.08
a. $300 - $275 = $25
b. $300 - $150 = ($150)
c. $100 - $95 = ($5)
d. $270 - $85 = $185
e. $400 - $80 = $320
f. $345 - $100 = $245
g. $25
h. $25 + ($150) = ($125)
i. ($125) + ($5) = ($130)
j. ($130) + $185 = $55
k. $55 + $320 = $375
l. $375 + $245 = $620

SELF TEST 2

2.01 e

2.20 d

2.03 a

2.04 g

2.05 f

2.06 b

2.07 c

2.08 a. Increase cash by $200.
b. Increase accounts receivable by $375.
c. Increase total assets by $575.
d. Increase investment by $575.
e. Increase total liabilities and owner's equity by $575.

2.09 a. $258.33 + $185.00 = $443.33
b. $3.75 + $105.86 + $47.33 + $106.19 + $213.15 + $49.75 = $526.03
c.
```
  $428.09
+  443.33
  -------
  $871.42
-  526.03
  -------
  $345.39
```
d. $428.09 - $3.75 = $424.34
e. $424.34 - $105.86 = $318.48
f. $318.48 - $47.33 = $271.15
g. $271.15 + $258.33 = $529.48
h. $529.48 - $106.19 = $423.29
i. $423.29 - $213.15 = $210.14
j. $210.14 + $185.00 = $395.14
k. $395.14 - $49.75 = $345.39

2.010 Income tax deduction = $450(0.14) = $63

Group health plan deduction = $4.25

Retirement plan deduction = $450(0.06) = $27

Social Security deduction = $450(0.0605) = $27.23

2.010 cont.

Total deduction = $63 + $4.25 + $27 + $27.23 = $121.48

Take-home pay per period = $450 - $121.48 = $328.52

2.011 Income tax deduction = $35(0.14) = $4.90

Retirement plan deduction = $35(0.06) = $2.10

Social Security deduction = $35(0.0605) = $2.12

Total deduction = $4.90 + $2.10 + $2.12 = $9.12

Take-home pay of raise = $35 - $9.12 = $25.88

SELF TEST 3

3.01 d

3.02 f

3.03 a

3.04 b

3.05 i

3.06 c

3.07 j

3.08 e

3.09 g

3.010 h

3.011 a. total costs
b. revenue

3.012 recession

3.013 a. price
b. production

3.014 Variable costs are costs directly affected by the number of units produced.

3.015 Yes, at least the portion that is not written off as bad debts. The rest will be paid for in cash, usually in 30 to 60 days.

3.016
a. \$300 - \$250 = (\$50)
b. \$350 - \$185 = \$165
c. \$300 - \$215 = \$85
d. \$350 - \$275 = \$75
e. \$400 - \$300 = \$100
f. \$550 - \$400 = (\$150)
g. (\$50)
h. (\$50) + \$165 = \$115
i. \$115 + \$85 = \$200
j. \$200 + \$75 = \$275
k. \$275 + \$100 + \$375
l. \$375 + (\$150) = \$225

CONSUMER MATHEMATICS 9
SELF TEST
SOLUTION KEY

SELF TEST 1

1.01 b

1.02 a

1.03 c

1.04 true

1.05 false

1.06 true

1.07 a.

b.

c.

1.08 a. $P = 2.5 + 6 + 0.5 + 4 + 4 + 0.5 + 6$
$= 23.5''$

b. $A_{rectangle} = 6(2.5) = 15 \text{ in.}^2$
$A_{triangle} = \frac{1}{2}(3.5)(3.6) = 6.30 \text{ in.}^2$

Total area $= 15 + 6.30 = 21.30 \text{ in.}^2$

1.09 $\frac{\frac{15}{15}}{\frac{45}{15}} = \frac{1}{3}$

1.010 $14:56::42:C$
$56 \times 42 = 14 \times C$
$2{,}352 = 14C$
$\frac{2{,}352}{14} = \frac{14C}{14}$
$C = 168$

1.011 $15:75 = \frac{15}{75} = \frac{1}{5}$ or $1:5$

1.012 Length:
14 ft. = 168 in.
$\frac{1}{4}:12 = l:168$
$12 \times l = \frac{1}{4} \times 168$
$12l = 42$
$\frac{12l}{12} = \frac{42}{12}$
$l = \frac{42}{12} = \frac{7}{2} = 3\frac{1}{2}''$

Width:
6 ft. = 72 in.
$\frac{1}{4}:12 = w:72$
$12 \times w = \frac{1}{4} \times 72$
$12w = 18$
$\frac{12w}{12} = \frac{18}{12}$
$w = \frac{18}{12} = \frac{3}{2} = 1\frac{1}{2}''$

Depth:
2 ft. = 24 in.
$\frac{1}{4}:12 = d:24$
$12 \times d = \frac{1}{4} \times 24$
$12d = 6$
$\frac{12d}{12} = \frac{6}{12}$
$d = \frac{6}{12} = \frac{1}{2}''$

1.013 $1:100{,}000 = 5:d$
$1 \times d = 100{,}000 \times 5$
$d = 500{,}000$
$= \frac{500{,}000}{5{,}280 \times 12}$
$= \frac{500{,}000}{63{,}360}$
$= 7.9$ miles

1.014 The lowest common denominator is 100; $\frac{1}{25} = \frac{4}{100}, \frac{4}{50} = \frac{8}{100}, \frac{8}{100} = \frac{8}{100}$, and $\frac{3}{25} = \frac{12}{100}$.

$$\frac{4}{100} + \frac{8}{100} + \frac{8}{100} + \frac{12}{100} = \frac{32}{100} = \frac{8}{25}$$

1.015

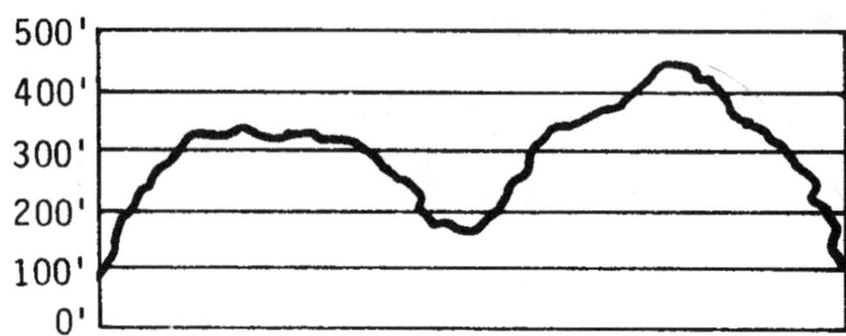

SELF TEST 2

2.01 false

2.02 true

2.03 true

2.04 false

2.05 true

2.06 a

2.07 c

2.08 b

2.09 b

2.010 d

2.011 c

2.012 a

2.013 f

2.014 b

2.015 d

2.016
$$\begin{aligned} C:3 &= 96:36 \\ C \times 36 &= 3 \times 96 \\ 36C &= 288 \\ \frac{36C}{36} &= \frac{288}{36} \\ C &= 8 \end{aligned}$$

2.017
$$\begin{aligned} 1:75{,}000 &= 7.5:d \\ 1 \times d &= 75{,}000 \times 7.5 \\ d &= 562{,}500 \\ &= \frac{562{,}500}{5{,}280 \times 12} \\ &= \frac{562{,}500}{63{,}360} \\ &= 9 \text{ miles} \end{aligned}$$

2.018
$$\begin{aligned} A &= 3.634(2.5)^2 \\ &= 3.634(6.25) \\ &= 22.7 \text{ in.}^2 \end{aligned}$$

2.019 $(8 - 2)180° = (6)180° = 1{,}080°$

2.020 Sum of interior angles of a square $= (4 - 2)180° = (2)180° = 360°$

Sum of interior angles of an octagon $= (8 - 2)180° = (6)180° = 1{,}080°$

$\frac{360°}{1{,}080°} = \frac{1}{3}$, so the answer is no.

2.021

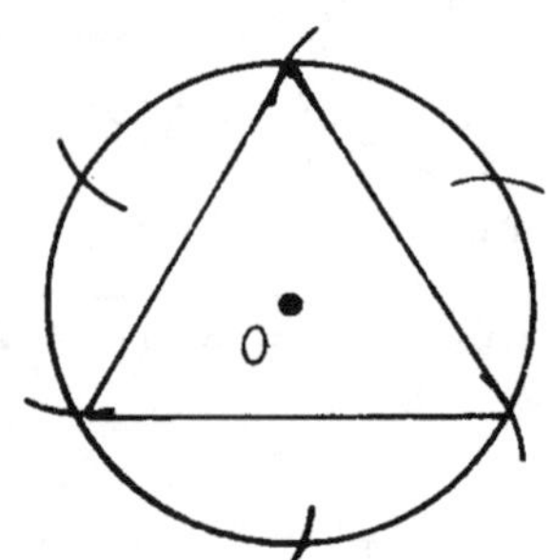

2.022 interior angle $= (1 - \frac{2}{5})180°$

$= (\frac{3}{5})180°$
$= 108°$

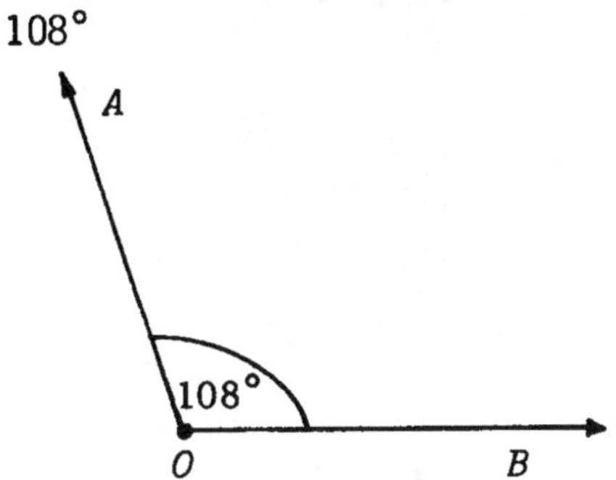

2.023

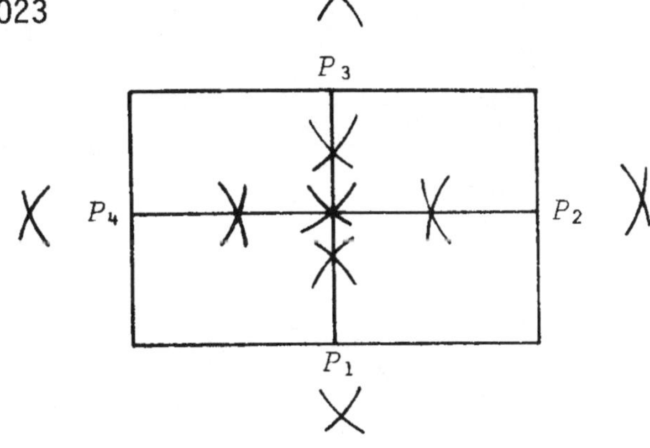

2.024

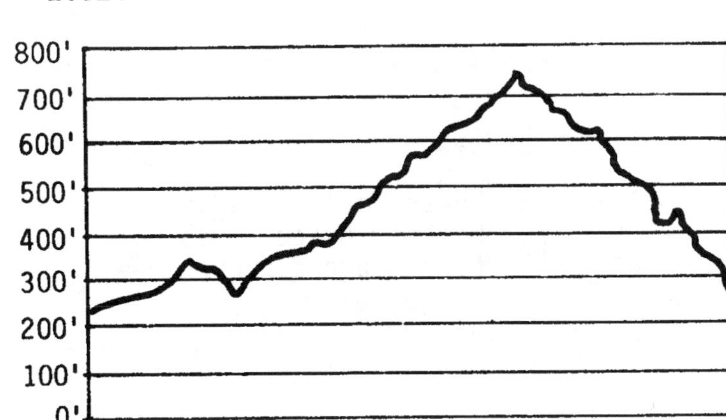

2.025

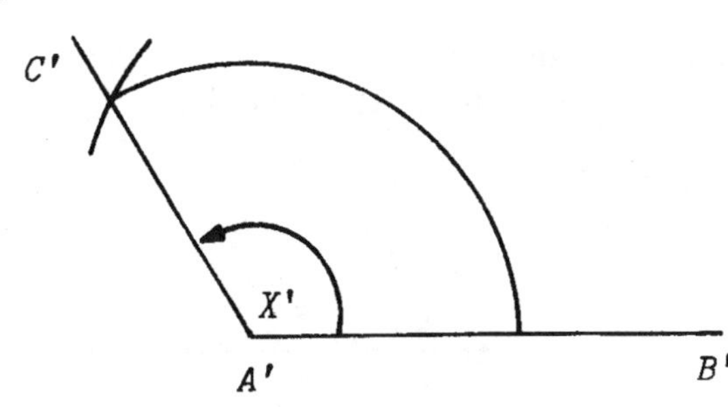

SELF TEST 3

3.01 through 3.06 Any order:

3.01 cork

3.02 vinyl

3.03 linoleum

3.04 acrilan

3.05 nylon

3.06 rayon

3.07 a sheet of graph paper

3.08 index point

3.09 lowest common denominator

3.010 ratio

3.011 equality between ratios

3.012 contours

3.013 perimeter

3.014 scale

3.015 5521

3.016 $A = \frac{1}{2}bh$

3.017 Any order:

a. acute; example:

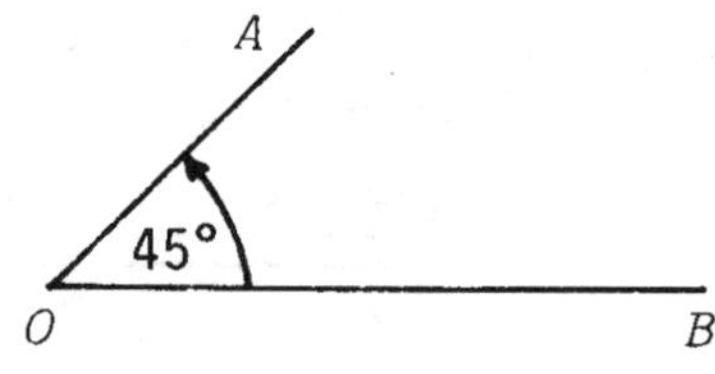

b. right; example:

c. obtuse; example:

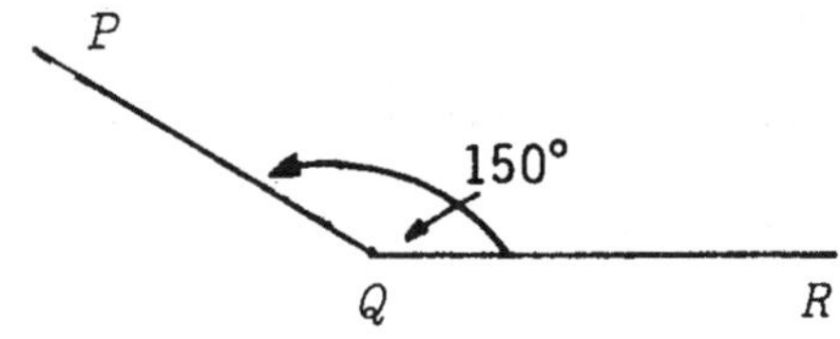

3.018

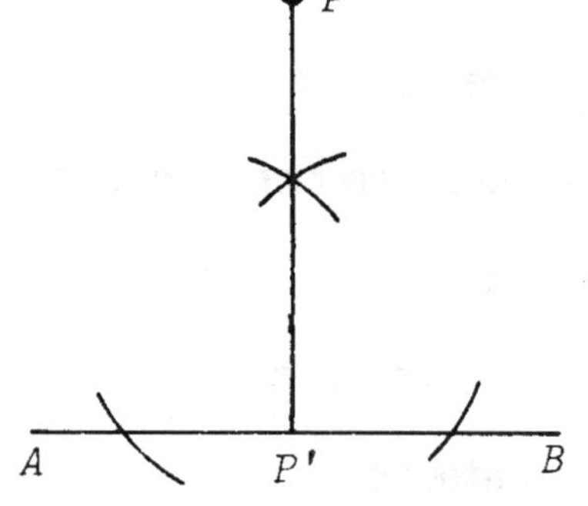

3.019
$$\begin{aligned} A &= 6.182(2\tfrac{1}{3})^2 \\ &= 6.182(\tfrac{7}{3})^2 \\ &= 6.182(\tfrac{49}{9}) \\ &= 33.7 \text{ in.}^2 \end{aligned}$$

3.020
$$\begin{aligned} A &= 10'6'' \times 11'9'' \\ &= 10.5' \times 11.75' \\ &= 123.375 \text{ ft.}^2 \\ &= \frac{123.375}{9} \\ &= 13.7 \text{ yd.}^2 \end{aligned}$$

3.021

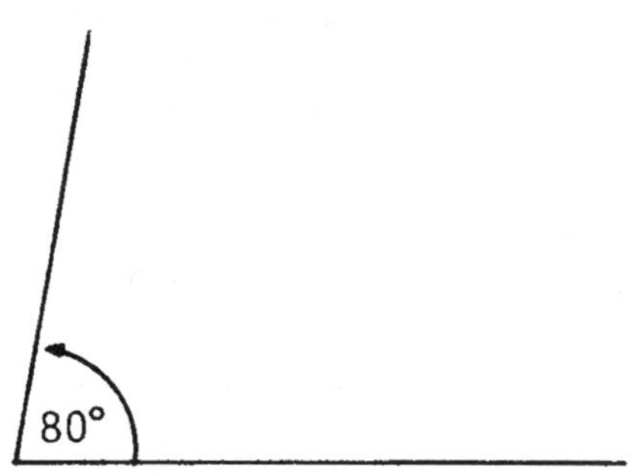

3.022

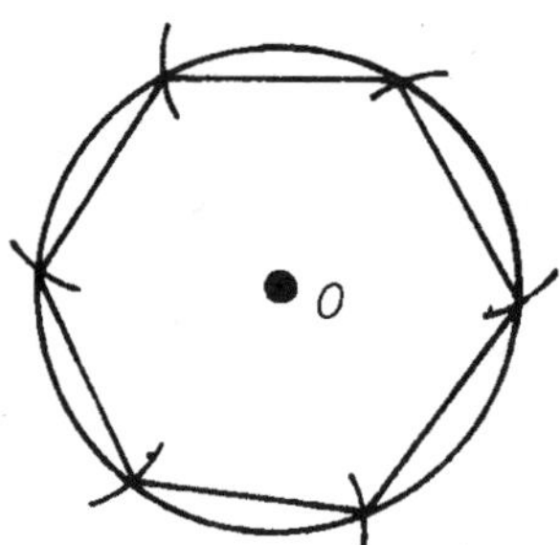

3.023 a. Lowest price = \$2.60

Highest price = \$15.00

Percentage difference =

$$\frac{\$15.00 - \$2.60}{\$2.60} = \frac{\$12.40}{\$2.60} = 4.77 = 477\%$$

3.023 cont.

b. Lowest price = \$15.00
Highest price = \$450.00
Percentage difference =
$\frac{\$450.00 - \$15.00}{\$15.00} = \frac{\$435.00}{\$15.00} = 29 = 2{,}900\%$

c. Lowest price = \$6.90
Highest price = \$225.00
Percentage difference =
$\frac{\$225.00 - \$6.90}{\$6.90} = \frac{\$218.10}{\$6.90} = 31.61 = 3{,}161\%$

3.024 Average price of acrilan carpet $= \frac{\$8.00 + \$22.50}{2} = \frac{\$30.50}{2} = \$15.25/\text{yd.}^2$

Average price of sponge rubber pad $= \frac{\$1.75 + \$6.00}{2} = \frac{\$7.75}{2} = \$3.88/\text{yd.}^2$

a. $A = 18.5 \times 21 = 388.5 \text{ ft.}^2 = \frac{388.5}{9} = 43.167 \text{ yd.}^2$
Cost of carpet = 43.167(\$15.25) = \$658.30
Cost of padding = 43.167•(\$3.88) = \$167.49
Total cost = \$658.30 + \$167.49 = \$825.79 for living room

3.024 cont.

b. $A = 10.5 \times 9.5 = 99.75 \text{ ft.}^2 = \frac{99.75}{9} = 11.083 \text{ yd.}^2$

Cost of carpet = 11.083(\$15.25) = \$169.02
Cost of padding = 11.083•(\$3.88) = \$43.00
Total cost = \$169.02 + \$43.00 = \$212.02 for dining room

c. $A = 25 \times 4.5 = 112.5 \text{ ft.}^2 = \frac{112.5}{9} = 12.5 \text{ yd.}^2$
Cost of carpet = 12.5(\$15.25) = \$190.63
Cost of padding = 12.5(\$3.88) = \$48.50
Total cost = \$190.63 + \$48.50 = \$239.13 for hallway

CONSUMER MATHEMATICS 10
SELF TEST
SOLUTION KEY

SELF TEST 1

1.01 a

1.02 b

1.03 d

1.04 c

1.05 b

1.06 a

1.07 d

1.08 c

1.09 c

1.010 scientific notation

1.011 denominators will divide evenly

1.012 invert the second fraction and multiply

1.013 changed to improper fractions

1.014 an exterior angle

1.015 $\frac{\frac{38}{2}}{\frac{84}{2}} = \frac{19}{42}$

1.016 $3\frac{20}{27} = \frac{3 \times 27 + 20}{27}$
$= \frac{81 + 20}{27}$
$= \frac{101}{27}$

1.017 $7:42 = c:36$
$1:6 = c:36$
$6 \times c = 1 \times 36$
$6c = 36$
$\frac{6c}{6} = \frac{36}{6}$
$c = 6$

1.018 $(n - 2)180° = 1{,}260°$
$180°n - 360° = 1{,}260°$
$180°n = 1{,}260° + 360°$
$180°n = 1{,}620°$
$\frac{180°n}{180°} = \frac{1{,}620°}{180°}$
$n = 9$

A nine-sided polygon is a nonagon.

1.019 $A = \pi ab$
$= 3.142(5)(3.5)$
$= 55 \text{ cm}^2$

1.020 $A = 4.828(4)^2$
$= 4.828(16)$
$= 77 \text{ cm}^2$

1.021 $90.85 = 3.634s^2$
$\frac{90.85}{3.634} = \frac{3.634s^2}{3.634}$
$25 = s^2$
$\sqrt{25} = \sqrt{s^2}$
$5 \text{ cm} = s$
$5 \text{ cm} = 5 \times \frac{1}{2.54}$
$= \frac{5}{2.54}$
$= 2 \text{ in.}$

1.022 2.85×10^7

1.023 $27\frac{3}{5}\% = 27.6\% = 0.276$

1.024 4 nanoseconds

1.025 $r_2 = \frac{1}{2}r_1$
$= \frac{1}{2}(6)$
$= 3''$

$A = \pi r^2$
$= 3.142(3)^2$
$= 3.142(9)$
$= 28.278 \text{ in.}^2$

1.026 Find the radius of the sphere.

$150 = 6s^2$

$\frac{150}{6} = \frac{6s^2}{6}$

$25 = s^2$

$\sqrt{25} = \sqrt{s^2}$

$5 \text{ in.} = s$

radius $= \frac{1}{2}(5) = 2.5$ in.

$V = \frac{4}{3}\pi r^3$
$= \frac{4}{3}(3.142)(2.5)^3$
$= \frac{4}{3}(3.142)(15.625)$
$= \frac{4}{3}(49.09375)$
$= 65.46 \text{ in.}^3$

SELF TEST 2

2.01 Any angle greater than 0° but less than 90°.

Example:

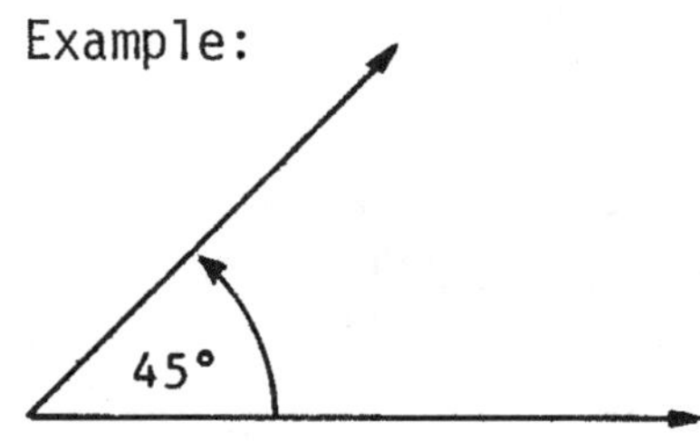

2.02

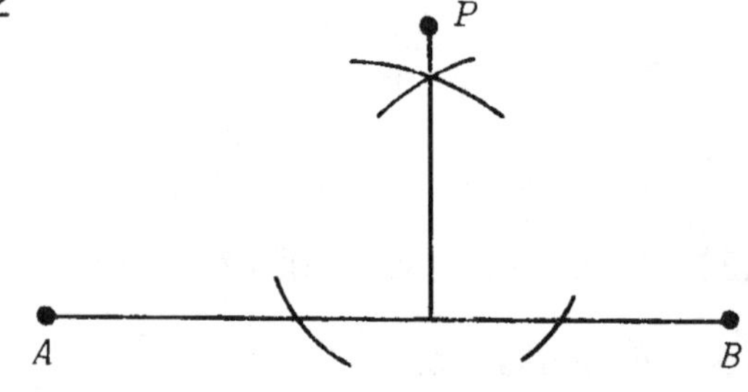

2.03 The lowest common denominator is 32.

$\frac{3}{8} + 2\frac{5}{16} + \frac{7}{8} + 4\frac{3}{32} + \frac{9}{16} + 5\frac{3}{4} =$

$\frac{3}{8} + \frac{37}{16} + \frac{7}{8} + \frac{131}{32} + \frac{9}{16} + \frac{23}{4} =$

$\frac{12}{32} + \frac{74}{32} + \frac{28}{32} + \frac{131}{32} + \frac{18}{32} + \frac{184}{32} =$

$\frac{447}{32} =$

$13\frac{31}{32}$

2.04 $\frac{9}{16} = 9 \div 16 = 0.5625 = 56.25\%$

2.05 $c:102 = 15:90$
$c:102 = 1:6$
$c \times 6 = 102 \times 1$
$6c = 102$
$\frac{6c}{6} = \frac{102}{6}$
$c = 17$

2.06 A number that contains a whole number and a fraction.

2.07 $\frac{16}{21} \div 2\frac{3}{7} =$

$\frac{16}{21} \div \frac{17}{7} =$

$\frac{16}{\cancel{21}_3} \times \frac{\cancel{7}^1}{17} = \frac{16}{51}$

2.08 $0.33\frac{1}{3} \times 600 =$
$\frac{1}{3} \times 600 = 200$

2.09 a. 7

b. $(1 - \frac{2}{7})180° =$

$(\frac{5}{7})180° = 128.6°$(approx.)

2.010 a. 5

b. $(1 - \frac{2}{5})180° =$

$(\frac{3}{5})180° = 108°$

2.011 a. 3

b. $(1 - \frac{2}{3})180° =$

$(\frac{1}{3})180° = 60°$

2.012 a. 12

b. $(1 - \frac{2}{12})180° =$

$(\frac{5}{6})180° = 150°$

2.013 true

2.014 true

2.015 false

2.016 false

2.017 true

2.018 b

2.019 a

2.020 c

2.021 d

2.022 a

2.023 c

2.024 a

2.025 b

2.026 g

2.027 d

2.028 f

SELF TEST 3

3.01 Any order:
a. term insurance
b. ordinary whole-life insurance
c. limited-payment insurance
d. endowment insurance

3.02 a. Tithe first.
b. Let God guide you as you spend the other nine tenths.
c. Determine fixed expenses.
d. Carefully estimate other expenses.
e. Plan a realistic budget.
f. Divide your paycheck according to the budget.
g. Do not spend money you do not have.

3.03 a. a number with a whole number and a fraction
b. a fraction with a numerator greater than its denominator giving it a value greater than 1
c. per hundred

3.04 Find in the chart the amount of \$1.00 at 2% per 40 years and multiply by \$200:

2.2080397 x \$200 = \$441.61

3.05

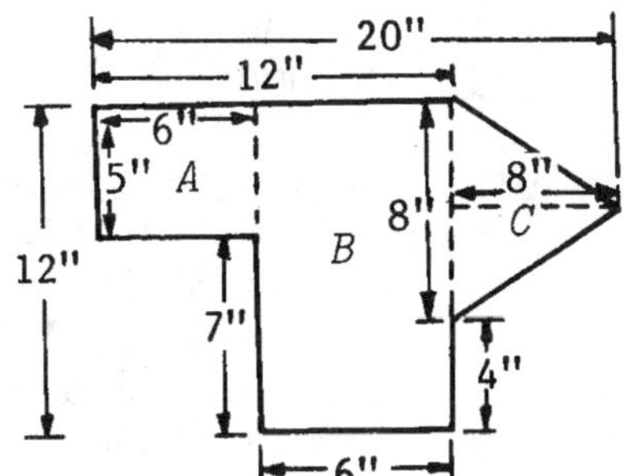

$A_A = 5 \times 6 = 30 \text{ in.}^2$

$A_B = 6 \times 12 = 72 \text{ in.}^2$

$A_C = \frac{1}{2} \times 8 \times 8 = 32 \text{ in.}^2$

Total area = 134 in.^2

3.06 FICA deduction =
$825 x 0.0605 = $49.91

Federal income tax deduction =
$825 x 0.14 = $115.50

State income tax deduction =
$825 x 0.02 = $16.50

Pension deduction =
$825 x 0.06 = $49.50

Charitable contribution deduction =
$825 x 0.015 = $12.38

Credit union savings plan deduction = $15

Total of deductions =
$49.91 + $115.50 + $16.50 + $49.50 + $12.38 + $15.00 = $258.79

Take-home pay = $825.00 - $258.79 = $566.21

3.07 Since one-way distance is 3,800 miles, round-trip distance is 2 x 3,800, or 7,600 miles.

a. $\frac{\$754.30}{7,600} = \$0.099 = 9.9¢/\text{mile}$

b. $\frac{\$775.20}{7,600} = \$0.102 = 10.2¢/\text{mile}$

3.08 a. $4,800,000,000 = 4.8 \times 10^9$ miles
$2,790,000,000 = 2.79 \times 10^9$ miles

b. $\frac{4,800,000,000 - 2,790,000,000}{2,790,000,000} =$
$\frac{2,010,000,000}{2,790,000,000} = 0.72 = 72\%$

3.09 a. Total Costs = Fixed Costs + Valuable Costs
= $3,525 + $3.25(1,500)
= $3,525 + $4,875
= $8,400

b. Profit = Revenue - Total Costs
= $8.95(1,500) - $8,400
= $13,425 - $8,400
= $5,025

CONSUMER MATHEMATICS 1
LIFEPAC TEST
SOLUTION KEY

1. $281 \times 94 = 26{,}414$

2. $834 \times 618 = 515{,}412$

3.
$$\begin{array}{r} 19 \\ \times\ 46 \\ \hline 114 \\ 76 \\ \hline 874 \end{array}$$

4.
$$\begin{array}{r} 34 \\ \times\ 23 \\ \hline 102 \\ 68 \\ \hline 782 \end{array}$$

5.
$$\begin{array}{r} 34 \text{ R1} \\ 7\overline{)239} \\ 21 \\ \hline 29 \\ 28 \\ \hline 1 \end{array}$$

6. The factors of 56 are 1, 2, 4, 7, 8, 14, 28, and 56. The largest prime factor is 7.

7. The factors of 34 are 1, 2, 17, and 34. The largest prime factor is 17.

8. $5 \times 7 \times 21 = 735$

9. $54 + 82 = 136$
$209 - 136 = 73$

10. $208 \div 8 = 26$

11. $10{,}224 \div 24 = 426$

CONSUMER MATHEMATICS 2
LIFEPAC TEST
SOLUTION KEY

1. $\frac{17}{2} \times \frac{7}{2} = \frac{119}{4}$

2. $17\overline{)47{,}300.0000}$ = 2,782.3529 = 2,782.353

```
      2,782.3529 = 2,782.353
17)47,300.0000
   34
   133
   119
    140
    136
      40
      34
       60
       51
        90
        85
         50
         34
         160
         153
```

3.

```
  42.300
-  1.094
  41.206
```

4. $\frac{1}{6} \times \frac{8}{3} = \frac{8}{18} = \frac{4}{9}$

5.

```
  0.0318
x    1.6
    1908
    318
 0.05088 = 0.051
```

6. $\frac{20}{24} - \frac{9}{24} = \frac{11}{24}$

7. $\frac{12}{39} + \frac{5}{39} = \frac{17}{39}$

8.

```
    4.1
    0.032
+ 147
  151.132
```

9. 38 ÷ 0.14 = 271.429

10. 463 x 0.91 = 421.33

11. 516 ÷ 1,042 = 0.495 = 49.5%

12. 14 ÷ 0.65 = 21.538

13. 43 x 0.25 = 10.75

14. 97 ÷ 140 = 0.693 = 69.3%

15. $640 \div \frac{1}{2} = 640 \times \frac{2}{1}$ = 1,280 plots

16. $14\frac{1}{2} + 3\frac{1}{4} = \frac{29}{2} + \frac{13}{4} = \frac{58}{4} + \frac{13}{4} = \frac{71}{4}$ dozen

17. $4\frac{1}{8} \div 7 = \frac{33}{8} \div \frac{7}{1} = \frac{33}{8} \times \frac{1}{7} = \frac{33}{56}$ foot

18. $3\frac{1}{8} - 1\frac{1}{2} = \frac{25}{8} - \frac{3}{2} = \frac{25}{8} - \frac{12}{8} = \frac{13}{8}$ yards

19.

```
  $ 2.25
x    4.5
    1125
    900
 $10.125 = $10.13
```

20.

```
        1.504 = $1.50
843)1,268.500
      843
      4255
      4215
        4000
        3372
```

21. 70 kilometers = 231,000 feet;
1 kilometer = 1,000 meters;
70 kilometers = 70,000 meters;
70 meters = 231 feet

22. $400 \div 640 = 0.625 = 62.5\%$

23. $\$11,250 \times 0.38 = \$4,275$

24.
$$\begin{array}{r} 3.112 \\ 475.3 \\ +\ 37 \\ \hline 515.412 \end{array}$$

25. $\$27.50 \times 0.05 = \$1.375 = \$1.38$

CONSUMER MATHEMATICS 3
LIFEPAC TEST
SOLUTION KEY

1. earnings paid by period, not hourly

2. every two weeks

3. a percentage of sales paid to salesmen

4. $307.69 x 52 = $15,999.88

5. $15,000 ÷ 24 = $625

6. Sue worked 30 hours.
30 x $4.10 = $123

7. $47\frac{1}{2} - 40 = 7\frac{1}{2}$ overtime hours
$47\frac{1}{2} + (\frac{1}{2} \times 7\frac{1}{2}) = 47\frac{1}{2} + (\frac{1}{2} \times \frac{15}{2}) = 47\frac{1}{2} + \frac{15}{4} = 51\frac{1}{4}$

8. Greg produced 822 units.
822 x 12¢ = $98.64

9. 0.165 x $4,736 = $781.44

10. $25,050 - $27,000 = ($1,950)

11. $37.10

12. 0.0605 x $398.00 = $24.08

13. 0.05 x $6.71 = $0.34

14. 0.016 x $6,000 = $96

15. a. $27.50 - $16.00 = $11.50
b. $11.50 ÷ $16.00 = 0.719 = 71.9%
c. $11.50 ÷ $27.50 = 0.418 = 41.8%

16. 55¢ ÷ 46 = 1.2¢ an oz.

6 x 10 = 60 oz.
75¢ ÷ 60 = 1.25¢ an oz.

The tomato juice at 1.2¢ an oz. (a) is more economical than the tomato juice at 1.25¢ an oz.

17. $11.00 x 20 = $220.00
$220.00 + $8.50 = $228.50
$228.50 - $200 = $28.50

18. By owner. Three bedroom home, family room, fireplace, den, large master bedroom.
7 rooms

19. Teacher check

CONSUMER MATHEMATICS 4
LIFEPAC TEST
SOLUTION KEY

1. b

2. h

3. a

4. e

5. g

6. d

7. i

8. f

9. c

10. Find the premium for a person aged 24 (27 - 3 = 24) under the "20-Year Endowment" column: $42.34.
$42.34 x 25 = $1,058.50

11. a. 27
b. $4.41 x 15 = $66.15

12. The man belongs to Class 2B.
a. $761.00 + $163.80 = $924.80
b. $976.96 + $196.60 = $1,173.56
c. $1,173.56 - $924.80 = $248.76

13. $104

14. $40,000

15. Add the outstanding checks:
$30.90 + $17.50 + $98.10 = $146.50
Subtract from the ending balance:
$378.19 - $146.50 = $231.69
Add the deposit:
$231.69 + $309.00 = $540.69
Subtract the service charge from the balance in the record book:
$544.90 - $4.21 = $540.69
No, an error does not exist.

16. a. Find in Figure 8 the amount of $1.00 at 6% for 25 years and multiply by $6,500:
4.2918707 x $6,500 = $27,897.16
b. $27,897.16 - $6,500 = $21,397.16
c. Find in the chart the amount of $1.00 at 3% for 50 years and multiply by $6,500:
4.3839060 x $6,500 = $28,495.39
d. $28,495.39 - $6,500 = $21,995.39
e. Find in the chart the amount of $1.00 at $1\frac{1}{2}$% for 100 years and multiply by $6,500:
4.4320457 x $6,500 = $28,808.30
f. $28,808.30 - $6,500 = $22,308.30

17. a. $50,000 ÷ 100,000 = $0.50
b. $0.50 x 25 = $12.50

18. Any four of these five examples:
a. He can neglect to make a will, in which case the law will dispose of his estate.
b. He can provide that he and his wife own all his property jointly.
c. He can make a will that distributes outright all of his estate to one or several named persons or institutions.
d. He can make a will leaving his estate in trust.
or
He can dispose of his estate by placing it in a living trust or by giving it away.

CONSUMER MATHEMATICS 5
LIFEPAC TEST
SOLUTION KEY

1. $100 = 10^2$
1 hectogram, 1 hg

2. $\frac{1}{10} = 10^{-1}$
1 decisecond, 1 ds

3. $150 \times 2.54 = 381$ cm

4. $1{,}500 \times \frac{1}{1.609} =$
$\frac{1{,}500}{1.609} =$
932.26 mi.

5. $15 \times 4.05 \times 10^{-1} =$
$15 \times 0.405 =$
6.075 or 6.08 hectares

6. $50 \times \frac{1}{2.59} =$
$\frac{50}{2.59} =$
19.31 mi.^{2}

7. $22 \times 3.785 = 83.27$ l

8. $8 \times 7.645 \times 10^{-1} =$
$8 \times 0.7645 =$
6.116 or 6.12 m^3

9. $2{,}000 \times 907.2 = 1{,}814{,}400$ kg

10. $°C = (653 - 32) \times \frac{5}{9}$
$= 621 \times \frac{5}{9}$
$= 345°C$

11. $A = 20 \times 25.5 = 510$ km^2

12. $A = \pi r^2$
$A = 3.14(6)^2$
$A = 3.14(36)$
$A = 113.04$ in.^{2}

13. $C = 2\pi r$
$280 = 2(3.14)r$
$280 = 6.28r$
$\frac{280}{6.28} = r$
$r = 44.58598$ cm
A (both ends) $= 2(\pi r^2)$
$= 2(3.14)(44.54343)^2$
$= 2(3.14)(1987.9096)$
$= 12{,}484.07$ cm^2

14. 6 in. $= \frac{1}{2}$ ft. or 0.5 ft.
Major semiaxis $= \frac{1}{2}(6) + 0.5$
$= 3 + 0.5$
$= 3.5$ ft.
Minor semiaxis $= \frac{1}{2}(4.5) + 0.5$
$= 2.25 + 0.5$
$= 2.75$ ft.

$A = \pi ab$
$A = \pi(3.5)(2.75)$
$A = 3.14(3.5)(2.75)$
$A = 30.22$ ft.^{2}

15. $V = 16 \times 12 \times 9 = 1{,}728$ cm^3

16. $V = \frac{1}{3}(6 \times 4)(8)$
$V = \frac{1}{3}(24)(8)$
$V = 64$ ft.^{3}

17. $A = 4\pi r^2$
$A = 4(3.14)(1)^2$
$A = 4(3.14)$
$A = 12.56$ in.^{2}

18. $A = \pi r\sqrt{r^2 + h^2}$
$A = 3.14(5)\sqrt{5^2 + 10^2}$
$A = 3.14(5)\sqrt{25 + 100}$
$A = 3.14(5)\sqrt{125}$
$A = 3.14(5)(11.18)$
$A = 175.5$ cm^2

19. $V = \pi abh$
$a = \frac{1}{2}(6) = 3$ cm
$b = \frac{1}{2}(5) = 2.5$ cm
$V = 3.14(2.5)(12)$
$V = 282.6$ cm^3

20. $A = 6a^2$
$A = 6(15)^2$
$A = 6(225)$
$A = 1350$ cm^2

CONSUMER MATHEMATICS 6
LIFEPAC TEST
SOLUTION KEY

1. $\$50.02 - 38.22 = \$11.80$

2. $\$4.65 \times 0.04 = \$0.186 = \$0.19$ tax
$\$4.65 + 0.19 = \$4.84$

3. Total payments made for 24 months = $42.50 x 24 = $1,020.

Total amount of interest = $1,020 - 850 = $170.

$y = 12$
$c = \$170$
$m = \$850$
$n = 24$

$$I = \frac{2(12 \times 170)}{850(24+1)} = \frac{2(2,040)}{850(25)} = \frac{4,080}{21,250} = 0.192$$
= 19.2%

4. $720(0.12) = $86.40

5. price = ($110 x .22) + $110
= $24.20 + $110
= $134.20

6. Area of dining room = 110 x 20 = 2,200 ft.^{2}

Area of kitchen and storage = $\frac{1}{3} \times 2,200 = 733\frac{1}{3}$ or 733 ft.^{2}

7. 48 x 250 = 12,000 ft.^{2}
Required area of garage = 2 x 12,000
= 24,000 ft.^{2}

8. $E = RI = 2(60) = 120$ volts

9. $$\frac{30}{\text{No. teeth gear 2}} = \frac{75}{150}$$
75(No. teeth gear 2) = 30(150)
$$\text{No. teeth gear 2} = \frac{30(150)}{75} = 30(2)$$
= 60 teeth

10.

weight$_1$ x distance$_1$ = weight$_2$ x distance$_2$

$150 \times 15 = 450 \times d_2$
$2,250 = 450d_2$
$$\frac{2,250}{450} = \frac{450d_2}{450}$$
$5 = d_2$
$d_2 = 5$ ft.

11. Since pulleys b and c are keyed together, the r.p.m. of pulley b = the r.p.m. of pulley c = 1,000 r.p.m.

$$\frac{d_c}{d_d} = \frac{\text{r.p.m.}_d}{\text{r.p.m.}_c}$$
$$\frac{6}{5} = \frac{\text{r.p.m.}_d}{1,000}$$
$$\frac{6(1,000)}{5} = \text{r.p.m.}_d$$
$$\frac{6,000}{5} = \text{r.p.m.}_d$$
r.p.m.$_d$ = 1,200 r.p.m.

12. $F \times d_h = W \times d_a$
$F \times 21 = 180 \times 3.5$
$21F = 630$
$$\frac{21F}{21} = \frac{630}{21}$$
$F = 30$ lb.

13. No. of oz. needed = 165 x 6
= 990 oz.

No. of cans required = $\frac{990}{45}$
= 22 cans

14. 48 x 2.5 = 120 patrons

15. Converted weight = 135 x 0.45
= 60.75 kg
Recommended protein intake = 60.75 x 1
= 60.75g

16. Calories used = weight x calorie-use factor for 8-min. mile
= 187 x 0.65
= 121.55 or 121.6 cal

17. Labor cost = $8.75 x 16
= $140
Total cost of services = $273
Overhead rate = $\frac{\$273 - 140}{\$140}$
= $\frac{\$133}{\$140}$
= 0.95
= 95%

18. warmer

19. 54° - 51° = 3° warmer

20. fourth, seventh, and eighth years

21. percentage = $\frac{57° - 54°}{57°}$
= $\frac{3°}{57°}$
= 0.053
= 5.3%

22. 50° + 52° + 51° + 54° + 53° + 57° + 54° + 54° + 55° + 56° = 536°

average daily temperature = $\frac{536°}{10}$
= 53.6° or 54°

23. Ratios of stopping distance to speed:

20 mph: $\frac{43}{20}$ = 2.15

30 mph: $\frac{79}{30}$ = 2.63

40 mph: $\frac{126}{40}$ = 3.15

40 mph is the first speed that the ratio of stopping distance to speed is greater than 3 to 1.

24. $\frac{251}{79}$ = 3.18
Yes, the stopping distance approximately triples.

25. $\frac{328 - 183}{328} = \frac{145}{328}$
= 0.44
= 44%

26. 60 and 70 mph: $\frac{328 - 251}{251} = \frac{77}{251}$
= 0.31 = 31%
50 and 60 mph: $\frac{251 - 183}{183} = \frac{68}{183}$
= 0.37 = 37%
40 and 50 mph: $\frac{183 - 126}{126} = \frac{57}{126}$
= 0.45 = 45%
30 and 40 mph: $\frac{126 - 79}{79} = \frac{47}{79}$
= 0.59 = 59%
20 and 30 mph: $\frac{79 - 43}{43} = \frac{36}{43}$
= 0.84 = 84%

The greatest percentage increase in stopping distance occurs between 20 and 30 mph (84%).

27. $\frac{\$4,500 - 500}{5} = \frac{\$4,000}{5}$
$= \$800$

28. $\frac{\$10,000 - 2,800}{6} = \frac{\$7,200}{6}$
$= \$1,200$

29. $\frac{\$8,150 - 3,000}{5} = \frac{\$5,150}{5}$
$= \$1,030$

30. $\frac{\$12,995 - 4,700}{8} = \frac{\$8,295}{8}$
$= \$1,036.88$

31. $\frac{\$2,685 - 685}{3.5} = \frac{\$2,000}{3.5}$
$= \$571.43$

CONSUMER MATHEMATICS 7
LIFEPAC TEST
SOLUTION KEY

1. $I = \frac{2(12)(360)}{2,400(25)}$
$= \frac{8,640}{60,000}$
$= 0.144$
$= 14.4\%$

2. $c = \$93.33 \times 36 - \$3,000$
$= \$3,359.88 - \$3,000$
$= \$359.88$

$I = \frac{2(12)(359.88)}{3,000(36 + 1)}$
$= \frac{2(12)(359.88)}{3,000(37)}$
$= \frac{8,637.12}{111,000}$
$= 0.078$
$= 7.8\%$

3. $0.18 = \frac{2(12)c}{(5,555 - 555)(42 + 1)}$
$0.18 = \frac{2(12)c}{5,000(43)}$
$\frac{0.18(5,000)(43)}{2(12)} = c$
$\frac{38,700}{24} = c$
$c = \$1,612.50$

Amount of monthly payment $= \frac{\$5,000 + \$1,612.50}{42}$
$= \frac{\$6,612.50}{42}$
$= \$157.44$

4. Total operating cost $= \$1,000 + \$800$
$= \$1,800$

Number of miles driven per year $= \frac{\$1,800}{\$0.085}$
$= 21,176$ miles

5. Total depreciation $= \$3,800 - \$1,250$
$= \$2,550$

Average yearly depreciation $= \frac{\$2,550}{6}$
$= \$425$

6. Total depreciation $= \$5,000 - \$3,800$
$= \$1,200$

Total operating cost $= \$1,200 + \$750 + \$250 + \$300$
$= \$2,500$

Operating cost $= \frac{\$2,500}{17,500}$
$= 0.143$
$= 14.3$¢ per mile

7. Policy A: $\$157 + \$75 + \$65 + \$22 + \$15 = \$334$
Policy B: $\$152 + \$82 + \$75 + \$30 + \$18 = \$357$
Policy C: $\$160 + \$78 + \$68 + \$20 + \$12 = \$338$

Policy A is the least expensive policy and Policy B is the most expensive policy.

Percentage of increase $= \frac{\$357 - \$334}{\$334}$
$= \frac{\$23}{\$334}$
$= 0.069$
$= 6.9\%$

8. Policy A's ratio $= \frac{\$157}{\$334}$
$= 0.470 = 47.0\%$

Policy B's ratio $= \frac{\$152}{\$357}$
$= 0.426 = 42.6\%$

Policy C's ratio $= \frac{\$160}{\$338}$
$= 0.473$
$= 47.3\%$

Policy B has the lowest ratio.

9. Policy *A*: \$157 + \$75 + \$65 = \$297
Policy *B*: \$152 + \$82 + \$75 = \$309
Policy *C*: \$160 + \$78 + \$68 = \$306

Policy *B* is the most expensive.

10. $d = rt$
$2{,}160 = r(4\frac{1}{2})$
$2{,}160 = r(4.5)$
$\frac{2{,}160}{4.5} = \frac{r(4.5)}{4.5}$
$r = 480$ mph

11.

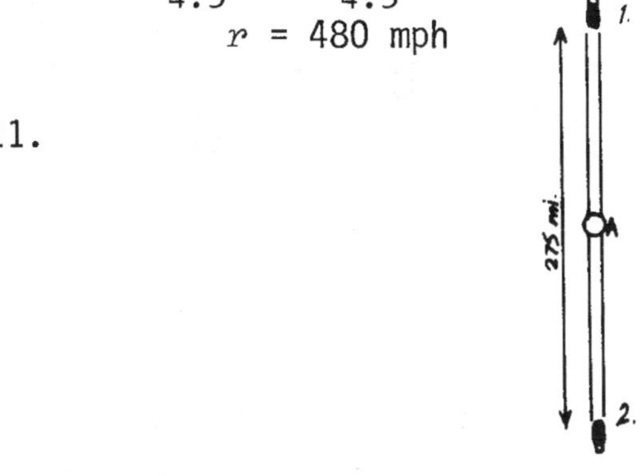

Car 1:
$d = rt = 35(4) = 140$ miles
Car 2:
$d = rt = 45(3) = 135$ miles

Total difference apart = 140 + 135
= 275 miles

12.

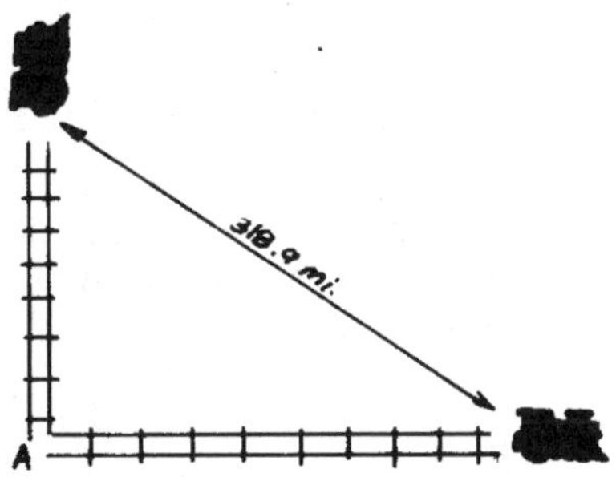

Train 1:
$d = rt = 60(4) = 240$ miles
Train 2:
$d = rt = 70(3) = 210$ miles

$(\text{distance apart})^2 = 240^2 + 210^2$
$= 57{,}600 + 44{,}100$
$= 101{,}700$
$\sqrt{(\text{distance apart})^2} = \sqrt{101{,}700}$
distance apart = 318.9 miles

13. Since neither Honolulu nor Tucson is on Daylight-Saving Time, the only time difference between the two cities is the standard time difference. The standard time difference is 3 hours (7 a.m. to 10 a.m.). Add 3 hours to 6:00 a.m.; the time in Tucson is 9:00 a.m.

14. The time difference between Cairo and Peking is 6 hours (7 p.m. to 1 a.m. the following day). Add 6 hours to 4 p.m.; the standard time in Peking is 10 p.m.

15. \$150(4.2937) = 644.06 bolivars

16. 1,500(.0337) = \$50.55

17. $\frac{2.73 - 2.20}{2.20} = \frac{0.53}{2.20}$
$= 0.241$
$= 24.1\%$

18. depreciated

19. Charter Group Air Fare = \$331.00
Charter Group Ship Fare = \$306.00

$\frac{\$331.00 - \$306.00}{\$306.00} = \frac{\$25.00}{\$306.00}$
$= 0.082$
$= 8.2\%$

20. Spain: \$14.51 - \$8.79 = \$5.72
Greece: \$16.55 - \$9.48 = \$7.07
Difference = \$7.07 - \$5.72
= \$1.35

21. $\frac{195.4 - 190.2}{190.2} = \frac{5.2}{190.2}$
$= 0.027$
$= 2.7\%$

22. 199.5 - 103.3 = 96.2

23. \$15(2) = \$30
\$30(20%) =
\$30(0.2) = \$6

CONSUMER MATHEMATICS 8
LIFEPAC TEST
SOLUTION KEY

1. false

2. true

3. false

4. true

5. true

6. adjusted price = (\$150 x .15) + \$150
= \$22.50 + \$150
= \$172.50

7. $\frac{\$85 - \text{adjusted price}}{\$85} = 0.12$

\$85 - adjusted price = \$85(0.12)
\$85 - adjusted price = \$10.20
adjusted price = \$85 - \$10.20
= \$74.80

8. adjusted price = \$135 - \$135(0.21)
= \$135 - \$28.35
= \$106.65

9. Let base price = x

\$176.50 = $.25x + x$

\$176.50 = $1.25x$

$\frac{\$176.50}{1.25} = x$ = \$141.20

10. $0.15 = \frac{\text{base price} - \$101.15}{\text{base price}}$

0.15(base price) = base price - \$101.15
0.15(base price) - base price = -\$101.15
base price - 0.15(base price) = \$101.15
base price(1 - 0.15) = \$101.15
base price(0.85) = \$101.15

10. cont.

$\frac{\text{base price}(0.85)}{0.85} = \frac{\$101.15}{0.85}$

base price = \$119

11. \$312.75 = \$278 (markup) + \$278

\$312.75 - \$278 = \$278(markup)

\$34.75 = \$278(markup)

$\frac{\$34.75}{\$278}$ = markup = .125

markup = 12.5%

12. \$133.45 = \$157 - \$157(% discount or markdown)

\$157 - \$133.45 = \$157(% discount or markdown)

\$23.55 = \$157(% discount or markdown)

$\frac{\$23.55}{\$157} = \frac{\$157(\%\text{ discount or markdown})}{\$157}$

% markdown or discount = 0.15; 15% discount or markdown.

13. c

14. a

15. d

16. b

17. c

18. $\frac{\$650}{\$15{,}000 - \$650} =$

$\frac{\$650}{\$14{,}350} =$

0.045 = 4.5%

19. $\frac{\$650}{\$15{,}000} = 0.043 = 4.3\%$

20. Total Costs = Fixed Costs + Variable Costs
= $6,500 + 1,500($19.50)
= $6,500 + $29,250
= $35,750

21. Profit = Revenue - (Fixed Costs + Variable Costs)
= $45,000 - ($11,000 + $22,500)
= $45,000 - $33,500
= $11,500

22. Profit = Revenue - (Fixed Costs + Variable Costs)
= $7,850($9.50) - ($8,000 + 10,000 x $5.75)
= $74,575 - ($8,000 + $57,500)
= $74,575 - $65,500
= $9,075

23. Price = $375(.75) + $375
= $281.25 + $375
= $656.25

24. $225 x 0.035 = $7.88
$225 - $7.88 = $217.12

25. Profit = Revenue - (Fixed Costs + Variable Costs)
$1,500 = Revenue - ($5,000 + $14,500)
$1,500 = Revenue - $19,500
$1,500 + $19,500 = Revenue
Revenue = $21,000

CONSUMER MATHEMATICS 9
LIFEPAC TEST
SOLUTION KEY

1. b
2. a
3. c
4. h
5. g
6. d
7. f
8. e
9. a
10. d
11. a
12. true
13. false
14. true
15. false
16. true

17. $C:16::6:8$
$C \times 8 = 16 \times 6$
$8C = 96$
$\frac{8C}{8} = \frac{96}{8}$
$C = 12$

18. The lowest common denominator is 24;
$\frac{1}{8} = \frac{3}{24}$, $\frac{2}{24} = \frac{2}{24}$, $\frac{5}{12} = \frac{10}{24}$, and $\frac{3}{8} = \frac{9}{24}$
$\frac{3}{24} + \frac{2}{24} + \frac{10}{24} + \frac{9}{24} = \frac{24}{24}$
$= 1$

19.

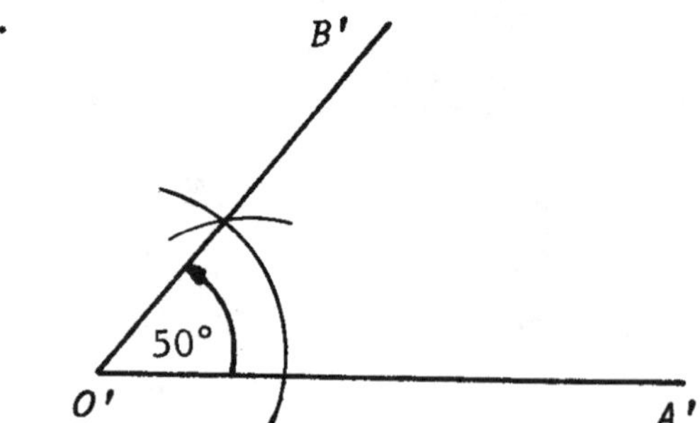

20. $A = 3.634(4)^2$
$= 3.634(16)$
$= 58 \text{ in.}^2$

21. Living room:
$A = 27 \times 9.5$
$= 256.5 \text{ ft.}^2$

Bedroom:
$A = 11 \times 9.5$
$= 104.5 \text{ ft.}^2$

Family room:
$A = 10.5 \times 11.5$
$= 120.75 \text{ ft.}^2$

Bathroom:
$A = 5 \times 7$
$= 35 \text{ ft.}^2$

Kitchen:
$A = 8.5 \times 10$
$= 85 \text{ ft.}^2$

Total floor area $= 256.5 + 104.5 + 120.75 + 35 + 85$
$= 601.75 \text{ ft.}^2$

22. a. $A = 120.75 \text{ ft.}^2$
$= \frac{120.75}{9}$
$= 13.42 \text{ yd.}^2$
Cost $= 13.42(\$5.00)$
$= \$67.10$

22. cont.

b. $A = 85 \text{ ft.}^2$

$= \frac{85}{9}$

$= 9.44 \text{ yd.}^2$

Cost = 9.44($2.60)

= $24.54

c. $A = 256.5 \text{ ft.}^2$

$= \frac{256.5}{9}$

$= 28.5 \text{ yd.}^2$

Cost = 28.5($5.50)

= $156.75

d. $A = 104.5 \text{ ft.}^2$

$= \frac{104.5}{9}$

$= 11.61 \text{ yd.}^2$

Cost = 11.61($5.50)

= $63.86

e. Total cost = $67.10 + $24.54 + $156.75 + $63.86

= $312.25

CONSUMER MATHEMATICS 10
LIFEPAC TEST
SOLUTION KEY

1. e
2. a
3. i
4. k
5. l
6. b
7. c
8. d
9. j
10. g
11. h
12. n
13. m
14. c
15. a
16.

$$64' = 768''$$
$$\frac{1}{32}:12 = l:768$$
$$12 \times l = \frac{1}{32} \times 768$$
$$12l = 24$$
$$\frac{12l}{12} = \frac{24}{12}$$
$$l = 2''$$

$$76' = 912''$$
$$\frac{1}{32}:12 = l:912$$
$$12 \times l = \frac{1}{32} \times 912$$
$$12l = \frac{57}{2}$$
$$\frac{12l}{12} = \frac{\frac{57}{2}}{12}$$
$$l = \frac{57}{24} = \frac{19}{8} = 2\tfrac{3}{8}''$$

16. cont.

$$80' = 960''$$
$$\frac{1}{32}:12 = l:960$$
$$12 \times l = \frac{1}{32} \times 960$$
$$12l = 30$$
$$\frac{12l}{12} = \frac{30}{12}$$
$$l = 2\tfrac{1}{2}''$$

$$28' = 336''$$
$$\frac{1}{32}:12 = l:336$$
$$12 \times l = \frac{1}{32} \times 336$$
$$12l = \frac{21}{2}$$
$$\frac{12l}{12} = \frac{\frac{21}{2}}{12}$$
$$l = \frac{21}{24} = \frac{7}{8}''$$

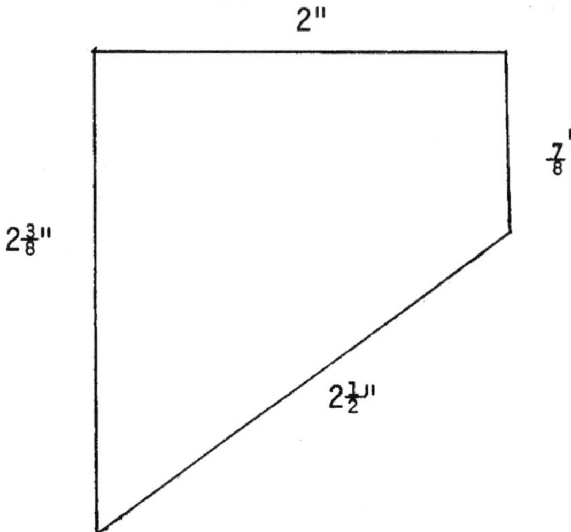

17. $A = \pi ab$
$= 3.142(10)(6)$
$= 188.52 \text{ cm}^2$

18. $0.28 \times 128 = 35.84$

19. $3\tfrac{5}{8} \times 16\tfrac{2}{5} =$

$$\frac{29}{\not{8}_4} \times \frac{\not{82}^{41}}{5} = \frac{1,189}{20} = 59\tfrac{9}{20}$$

20. 3 million = 3 x 10^6

$$\frac{9.27 \times 10^{27}}{3 \times 10^6} =$$

$$\frac{9.27}{3} \times 10^{27-6} = 3.09 \times 10^{21}$$

or

$$\frac{9,270,000 \times 10^{21}}{3,000,000} = 3.09 \times 10^{21}$$

21. $A = 2.598s^2$
$= 2.598(6)^2$
$= 2.598(36)$
$= 93.528$ or $93.53\ cm^2$

22. $\frac{\$2,800,000}{\$96,500,000} = 0.029 = 2.9\%$

23. 0.0521 x 100,000 = $5,210

24. 1,609 x 1.609 = 2,588.881 km/hr.
$= \frac{2,588.881}{60 \times 60}$
$= \frac{2,588.881}{3,600}$
= 0.72 km/sec.

25. $533.48 - $15.41 = $518.07

26. $518.07 + $39.82 = $557.89

27. $557.89 - $59.93 = $497.96

28. $497.96 - $10.02 = $487.94

29. $487.94 - $0.60 = $487.34

30. $487.34 + $41.10 = $528.44

31. $528.44 - $20.63 = $507.81

32. $507.81 - $11.41 = $496.67